THE BLEEDING SOCIETY

BENEDETTA WASONGA

Dedication

Hakesi was 50 years old when she died of untold circumstances. Unmarried with a daughter at the time of her death, and with the society's strict adherence to traditions, Hakesi was buried at the edge of the fence of her father's piece of land. The only send off they deemed fit since unmarried women were seen as a curse in society and hence not entitled to the family inheritance or a proper final resting place.

This book is dedicated to her.

Preface

Though human rights can be commonly understood as those rights which are inherent in human beings, and are protected by various national, regional and international frameworks, the pains and the unfathomable sufferings in societies continue in total disregard to these instruments and blatant disrespect to the rule of law by the same states who are signatories to these instruments.

Grisly cultural practices such as sexual cleansing and widow inheritance, Female Genital Mutilation (FGM); political exclusion and sometimes extermination of political opponents, gender inequalities, being denied of a nationality, unequal distribution of resources and in some cases obvious human rights violations coming from family members, people, institutions, governments which should be protecting its own citizens continue to happen.

The Universal Declaration of Human Rights; one of the oldest documents on human rights declares that all human beings are born free and equal in dignity and rights. They are endowed with reason and conscience and should act towards one another in a spirit of brotherhood.

Human rights denote all those rights which are inherent in our nature and without which we cannot live as human beings. Human rights as such are incorporated in various National and International Human Rights instruments such as the Convention on the Elimination of all Forms of Discrimination Against Women (CEDAW), Civil and Political Rights, Regional Human Rights treaties such as the African Charter on Human and Peoples Rights.

Despite all these, society still continues to bleed. Women and girls in this present era continue to undergo cultural practices that demean their existence, children continue to experience sufferings that should have otherwise been avoided, and girls continue to be married off to older men enough to be their grandfathers against the Convention on the Rights of a Child.

The Bleeding Society highlights the various sufferings and human rights violations that societies go through in the various parts of the world. It goes deep into analyzing different aspects of human rights violations that otherwise would have been avoided. The book is assumed to further the goal of a just and equitable society.

I would like to express my gratitude to all those who gave me advice, support and encouragement during the accomplishment of this book. I am indebted to all my family, friends and colleagues who directly or indirectly supported me to complete this book.

Writing this book has made me go through a learning curve. It has made me realize that making a contribution to society is not only achievable by my long term desire to work with the United Nations, the African Union, IGAD or any other International organization working towards the realization of human rights, rule of law, democracy and gender equality such as the Austrian Development Agency, Amnesty International and Open Society Foundations, that it is also achievable in my own little way through writing to address issues and reach to people who may be oblivious to the happenings in societies and in other parts of the world. It has fulfilled my long term passion, desire and ambition to make a contribution to humanity by way of highlighting the issues affecting societies.

The suffering of women, boys and girls, people with disability and refugees all over the world and the real life experiences highlighted in this book are a perfect example that life though unfair at times, the clock continues to tick and the responsible organs charged with the protection of human kind ought to act in haste.

It has made me realize how little I know about the most fascinating regions of the world where I lived or visited. I commit myself to continue learning.
Author

CONTENTS

CHAPTER 1
BORN STATELESS

"To be without a nationality is like you don't exist, you simply don't exist. You are faceless, nameless, unidentifiable and invisible and live in a world with no proof of your identity" – Leal

Deprived of a nationality and denied of their basic human rights, stateless people all over the world cannot access education, get into formal employment, open and operate bank accounts, own property such as land, move and travel freely or exercise their democratic rights such as the right to vote, also known as suffrage. The right to a nationality is of paramount importance to the realization of other fundamental existing human rights. Persons who lack a nationality or an effective citizenship are thus among the world's most vulnerable and at risk to human rights violations.

It is estimated that 10 million people globally do not have a nationality of any country. This is according to the United Nations out of which 680,000 are in Europe while thousands of them living in Africa who find themselves "non-persons" (a person regarded as non-existent or unimportant, or as having no rights; an ignored or forgotten person) in the only country they have lived and always known as home, although experts say the figure is more likely to be much higher. There are hundreds of thousands of Russian-speaking minorities in Latvia and Estonia who became non-citizens following the collapse of the Soviet Union. There exists thousands of Roma in Italy and Balkans left stateless as a result of the breakup of Yugoslavia.

In Myanmar, the 1.1 million Rohingya Muslims often called as the most marginalized and persecuted minority on earth are stateless and unwanted. This figure is according to the United Nations High Commissioner for Refugees (UNHCR). Neither Bangladesh nor will Myanmar grant them nationality as the Myanmar government considers them as undocumented immigrants.

Although perceived as a problem affecting a small minority of the global population, statelessness remains a significant yet poorly documented problem in Africa. The African Union estimates there are thousands of people across the continent that are presently stateless or at a threat of statelessness.

There are two main reasons for this state of affairs: During the colonial era, scores of people were brought into various countries in the African continent to work as casual labourers on plantations and did not receive nationality when the host countries gained self-determination. Their offspring still have no nationality despite having been in the country for many generations. The other is because there is no provision in national laws that bestow nationality to abandoned children. The United Nations High Commission for Refugees (UNHCR) estimates that there are 300,000 stateless people living in Côte d'Ivoire because of these reasons.

Of the states in Africa which still discriminate against women in their ability to pass on nationality to their children, nine are in sub-Saharan Africa and many African States do not have legislations that guarantee nationality to children born in their territory who would otherwise be stateless, as a result, children continue to be born stateless across Africa.

Internally Displaced Persons (IDPs), including refugees, are at a higher risk of losing their connection with their country of origin as well as facing challenges in acquiring documentation, which may result in statelessness.

Typically people acquire a nationality automatically at birth, either through their parents or the country in which they were born. Sometimes, however, a person must apply to become a national of a country.

The international legal definition of a stateless person according to the United Nations Convention on Stateless People is "a person who is not considered as a national by any State under the operation of its law".

In simple terms, this means that a stateless person does not have a nationality of any country anywhere in the world. Some people are born stateless, but others become stateless.

Looking at international law, there are two treaties that give specific protections for stateless persons, namely, the 1954 Convention on

Stateless Persons and the 1961 Convention on the Reduction of Statelessness. While these treaties provide considerable protections to stateless persons, the main test to their implementation is the lack of will of state participation. Article 15 of the Universal Declaration of Human Rights states that "everyone has the right to a nationality" and that "no one shall be arbitrarily deprived of his nationality nor denied the right to change his nationality." This includes both men and women.

In the African continent, member states are presently in the process of drafting a Protocol to the African Charter on Human and Peoples Rights on the Specific aspects on the Right to Nationality and Eradication of Statelessness in Africa. Despite the incompleteness of the Charter, the African Commission on Human and Peoples' Rights, by a bold interpretation of the

Charter has tried to limit the flexibility of States Parties tempted to use their national laws to deprive persons of their nationality.

According to UNHCR, The UN Refugee Agency, gaps in nationality laws are a major cause of statelessness. Each country has laws which establish the conditions somebody acquires nationality or can have it taken away. If these laws are not cautiously written and properly applied, some people may end up being excluded and left without a nationality. A perfect example is children who are of unknown parentage in a country where nationality is acquired based on descent from a national. Fortunately, most nationality laws recognize them as nationals of the state in which they are found, however the problem comes in when such a person is not able to prove his existence in that particular country.

Another aspect that contributes to statelessness comes in when people move from the countries where they were born. A child born in a foreign country risks becoming stateless if that country does not permit nationality based on birth only and if the country of origin does not allow either parent to pass on nationality through family ties. Additionally, the rules setting out who can and who cannot pass on their nationality are sometimes discriminatory. The laws in 27 countries do not let women pass on their nationality, while some countries limit citizenship to people of certain races and ethnicities. In contrast, men in these countries have nearly no obstacles to pass citizenship to their non-citizen spouse and children. These limitations are widespread in the Middle East and North Africa. In Jordan, for example, the law prohibits women married to non-citizens from passing citizenship to their children.

Another significant basis is the creation of new states and alteration in state boundaries. In many cases, particular groups can be left out without a nationality as a result and even where new countries permit nationality for all, tribal, ethnic, racial and religious minorities often have difficulty proving their connection to the country. In countries where nationality is only acquired by descent from a national, statelessness will be passed on to the next generation.

Finally, statelessness could possibly be caused by withdrawal or deprivation of nationality. In some countries, citizens can lose their nationality merely from having resided outside their country for a long period of time. States can also deprive citizens of their nationality through changes in laws that leave whole populations stateless, using discriminatory criteria like ethnicity or race.

In the Bahamas, the law makes it easier for men with foreign wives than for women with foreign husbands to pass on citizenship to their children, according to the State Department's Human Rights Report. And in Kiribati, an island nation in the Pacific Ocean, non-citizen wives automatically are granted citizenship through their husbands, while women who marry foreigners are not given that same advantage.

Sarah

Born and raised in the Democratic Republic of Congo (DRC) Sarah until the age of 18 possessed both Congolese and Rwandan nationality as her father is Rwandan and her mother is Congolese.
In august 1998 the Congo second war began, also known as the Great War of Africa or the Great African War, and sometimes referred to as the African World War little more than a year after the First Congo War. The war was between Rwanda and the Democratic Republic of Congo formerly known as Zaire although many other African countries were involved. While officially

the Southern African Development Community (SADC) members are bound to a mutual defence treaty in the case of outside attack, many member nations took an impartial stand to the conflict. However, the governments of Namibia, Zimbabwe and Angola supported the Kabila government after a meeting in Harare, Zimbabwe, on 19 August. Several more nations joined the conflict for Kabila in the subsequent weeks including Chad, Libya and Sudan.

In 2001, during the conflicts between the two neighboring countries, Sarah's parents were arrested on allegations of spying on the Congolese government. At the age of 15 Sarah was left on her own. She stayed with family friends for a year, but soon realized that she had nowhere to go without any relatives of her knowledge around to assist. More and more she felt that her life was in danger if she stayed in Congo.

After a year of her parents being put to jail, in 2002, when Sarah was only 16 years old, she fled to the Netherlands. On her arrival she applied for a residence permit for unaccompanied minor asylum seekers.

Her application was rejected and the process of repatriation commenced. However two days prior to her return to Kinshasa, Congo the Dutch Repatriation & Departure Service announced that the *Laisser-Passer* needed for her deportation and formerly granted by the Congolese authorities had been withdrawn for unknown reasons. This suspended the deportation process and Sarah was allowed to stay.

In order to legalize her status Sarah applied for a Dutch "no-fault residence permit", a one year residence permit for those who cannot leave the Netherlands through no fault of their own. As part of her application she had to acquire proof of identity documentation from the Congolese authorities and it was at this point Sarah for the first time realized that she was stateless.

The Congolese Embassy in the Netherlands stated that she automatically lost her Congolese nationality at the age of 18, stating that people with dual nationality are ought to opt for one nationality when they turn 18. Sarah was not aware of this.

She contacted the Rwandan Embassy several times to try and obtain identity documents from them. However, she was told that she cannot be recognized as Rwandan citizen because she was not born in Rwanda, and has no close links to the country.

"I'm staying irregularly in the Netherlands, no perspective of reacquiring a Congolese nationality or obtain the Rwandan nationality I thought I was entitled to".

Presently, twelve years later, Sarah is still stuck in the same situation, unable to acquire or re-acquire original Congolese or Rwandan identification documents. Since the Netherlands currently has no procedure to recognize or regularize stateless persons, Sarah's fate hanged in the balance.

"As I was in the process of applying for a residence permit for unaccompanied minor asylum seekers in the Netherlands, at least I had the chance to study and make friends. Right now I feel isolated; I stay at home every day. I wish I could start a family but I cannot."

Issa

Born in Kosovo former Yugoslavia, Issa fled to Belgrade following the 1999 war, but since he lacked any legal documentation to prove his identity, it was not possible for him to be registered as a refugee nor an internally displaced person (IDP).

His very first document, his birth certificate, was issued in 2013 when he was 29. Yes you got it right... 29. This was only possible due to a new procedure introduced in 2012 that allowed displaced people and refugees acquisition of a birth certificate. Up till then Issa lived a life of an indiscernible. He did not attend school, he did not have health insurance and the only pieces of evidence about his residence are the statements of his common-law wife and his neighbours.

"Not possessing a national identity card is the worst... I feel as if I am different for not having legal documents, and people certainly see me in a different way because of it. They think I am a criminal."

Even though he managed to register his birth with the birth registry, Issa remains stateless with no nationality. He cannot "inherit" his father's nationality since his father doesn't have any (his father was born in Macedonia and lived in Kosovo since the 1980s, but has never had his nationality formally registered) or his mother's (she left Issa when he was only two weeks old and Issa doesn't know if she held any nationality at the moment of his birth). Without nationality, Issa remains deprived of basic human rights.

"I cannot marry, recognize paternity of my children, as well as visit my family in Kosovo. I cannot work lawfully, get social welfare support or register for health cover. To be without legal papers and a nationality is as if you don't exist in this world".

Serbia presently lacks policies and regulations to recognize Issa's statelessness and legalize his status. In the interim, the only option open to him at present is to attempt to obtain Serbian nationality through the naturalization process. Unfortunately, the result of the process remains in doubt as Issa cannot furnish any documentary evidence of his residence, which is one of the legal requirements. So he remains trapped in a vicious loop and facing a life in limbo.

"I am terrified of the police since I don't have papers. I hope it will be better and different in the future and I hope to attain a nationality. I believe I would feel better then because I would be able to live with no fear".

The Story of the Makonde

"The day I got my Kenyan identity card I came home and celebrated. I'm now a "proper" Kenyan. I can go anywhere and get assistance without any fear or discrimination."-Khadija Mrisho.

Khadija is amongst the over 1,000 Makonde community in Kenya who were issued with Kenyan identity cards in 2017 when the

Makonde were formally declared the 43rd tribe in Kenya by President Kenyatta.

Her parents were born in Kenya and she is a third generation Makonde. Her grandparents settled in Kenya from Mozambique to work in sisal plantations in the coastal region of Kenya.

The story is similar for many from the Makonde community in Kenya. Their forefathers hailed from Mozambique and arrived in Kenya through Tanzania in the early 1930s to work for the British colonialist. They had on no account been acknowledged as Kenyans. They were stateless.

"We had legal rights but we did not have the opportunity to enjoy these rights since we did not have Kenyan National identity cards. We have suffered."-Khadija

Without Kenyan national identity cards, the Makonde could not open and operate bank accounts, register for telephone services, obtain business licenses and permits to conduct business, travel freely or even register for mobile banking services by various banks.

Known for carving wood as their main economic activity, an expertise they inherited from their forefathers, the Makonde's were exploited by middlemen for generations merely for the reason that they did not have Kenyan National identity cards a situation that has since changed.

"We are glad now that we have identity cards as proof of Kenyan nationality. We used to hide in the villages and caves since we could not conduct any business in town without permits." -Damiano Garcias.

Without national identity cards, the Makonde youth were discriminated against when applying for formal employment or joining youth groups.

As the Makonde celebrate the gains made in acquiring Kenyan nationality, they cannot help but empathize with other people who are stateless. They know too well the importance of having a nationality and the pains of being stateless.

Other than the Makonde, there are other stateless communities residing in Kenya such as the Pemba, the Shirazi, the Rundi and the Shona.

Everyone has a right to a nationality.

CHAPTER 2
CHILD BRIDE

"I am just a child not a wife, pay my school fees not bride price, say no to early marriages; Keep girls in school"-Unknown.

Child marriage is a problem all over the world. Each year, over 12 million girls are forcibly married off before attaining the age of 18. That is one girl every 2 seconds. According to the 2017 UNICEF report, State of the World's Children, the countries with the highest rates of child marriage before the age of 18 are Niger at 76%, Bangladesh at 59%, Mali at 52% and India at 48%. Out of the 25 countries with the highest rates of child marriage globally, almost all are affected by wars, fragility or natural disasters.

Although child marriage is common in the developing countries, far less well-known is the prevalence of the practice in America and nearly always among girls. The country's diplomats are dynamic in global efforts to outlaw it abroad, but American children are still allowed to marry albeit, more often than not, with parental approval and the endorsement of a judge. No American state has conceded a law that categorically forbids the practice. In a survey of marriage licenses compiled by Unchained At Last, at least 167,000 children under the age of 18 were married between the years 2000 and 2010. Unchained At Last, a non-governmental organization fighting against forced and arranged marriages, claimed while most states set the minimum marriage at 18, every state allows minors to get married through exceptions. In many states, 16 and 17 year olds can get married with approval from judge or their parents.

The practice is the noxious product of extreme poverty and gender inequality mostly in Africa and Asian countries. Girls in child marriages have a propensity to be less educated, and they are more likely to live in rural areas for the rest of their lives. Many poor parents believe that marrying off their girls will secure their daughters' future by ensuring that another family will be responsible for their upkeep and care and by extension to the girl's family. This also is true in humanitarian crises, when the fear of many parents is the inability to protect or care for their daughters. Some mistakenly believe marriage will protect their daughters from sexual violence, which is commonly exacerbated during armed conflicts and wars.

Some parents perceive their daughters as burdens or property. Bride price or dowry complicates the issue: In places where the bride's family pays dowry to the groom's family, younger brides usually command lesser price, creating an inducement for parents to marry off their daughters early. In areas where the groom's family pays a bride price, parents in difficult situations may marry off their daughters as a means of income or out of poverty.

More often than not, child marriage is the outcome of limited available choices. When girls have an option, most choose to marry later and pursue their education first or other aspirations.

Despite the fact that awareness around the problem of child marriage is increasing, for many people the million dollar question is still how it is happening? How is it that, in the 21st century, girls are still finding themselves being married off at such a young age when they should be in school learning and playing in fields? The practice is rampant in Kenya due to poverty, hunger, religious and cultural practices, gender inequality and lack of awareness. In some parts, parents marry off their children at a young age for prestige, baseless fears of getting pregnant out of wedlock and while at their fathers' homes. In some cases, parents reach into agreement with the families of men who sexually assault their daughters so that both families save their faces from the same of rape and or defilement.

Child marriage is a formal or informal union entered into by an individual before attaining the lawfully set marriageable age. It denies girls their right to make vital decisions about their sexual health and well-being. It forces them out of education and into a life of poor prospects, with an increased risk of violence, abuse, ill health or early death.

Going to school gives girls choices and opportunities in life, it aids their mental growth giving them a better chance and understanding of life and aspects it holds. Allowing them to play an active role in their communities and break the cycle of poverty. Girls who are married are unlikely to be in school as it depends on the spouse they get, whether supportive to educate her, but more often than not, they are expected to stay home and raise families. Education is essential for girls to be able to make informed decisions about their sexual health and well-being.

Despite being prohibited by international law, this harmful practice remains widespread. It continues to rob millions of girls under the age of 18 around the world of their childhood. Child marriage or marriage without the free and full consent of both spouses is a human rights violation and is not in line with international and regional agreements that provides protection to children against child marriages which include but not limited to the Universal Declaration of

Human Rights, Convention on the Elimination of Discrimination Against Women (CEDAW), Convention on Consent to Marriage, Minimum Age for Marriage and Registration of Marriage, Convention on the Rights of the Child, African Charter on the Rights and Welfare of the Child.

These instruments call for a uniform age of marriage and emphasize the importance of free, full and informed consent to marriage. The Convention on the Rights of a Child recommends that the minimum age of marriage be 18 years old, while Convention on the Elimination of Discrimination Against Women (CEDAW) obligates States to ensure on the basis of equality between men and women, the right to freely choose a spouse and enter into marriage only with free and full consent. Governments should adhere to in protecting children from being married before they are ready.

Child marriages more often than not happen outside the law, in rural areas with few resources to implement the law. Of 198 countries in the world, almost all (192) have laws that specify the minimum age one can legally marry. Six including Equatorial Guinea, Gambia, Saudi Arabia, Somalia, South Sudan and Yemen do not specify a minimum age for marriage.

The Nigerian Constitution does not ascertain the minimum age of marriage for both boys and girls. The Child Rights Act, which was passed in 2003, sets the age of marriage at 18 years-old although statistics by UNICEF report in 2017 show that 43% of girls are married off before their attain the age of 18 while 17% are married off before they celebrate their 15th birthday. Education is a strong indicator of whether a girl will marry as a child or not. 82% of women with no education were married before the age of 18, as opposed to

13% of women who had at least finished secondary education.

Global child marriage rates are progressively declining. Recent figures show that 25 million child marriages were prevented in the last decade. Around 2000, one in three women between the ages of 20 and 24 reported they had been married as children. In 2018, this number is around one in five.

However, progress has not been consistent, and the rate of child marriage is not declining fast enough. Due to population growth in regions where child marriage is more common, the total number of child marriages is projected to increase by 2030.

Ending child marriage requires action by various stakeholders at many levels. Existing laws against child marriage should be enforced, especially when girls who are in danger of child marriage, or who are already married,

seek for protection and justice. And where it is
not yet the case, the legal age of marriage should
be raised to 18 to conform to the definition of a
child as provided by various legislations and
international instruments. But laws only provide
the framework for action against child marriage.
Practices people deem culturally acceptable are
unlikely to wane through legislation alone.

Governments, civil society and other partners
must work together to ensure girls have access
to quality education at all levels, health
information and services, and life-skills training.
Girls who are able to stay in school and remain
healthy enjoy a broader range of options
available for them, and they are more likely to
avoid child marriage.

Importantly and not to be ignored, girls who are
already married need to be supported. Married
girls need reproductive health services to help
them avoid early and unplanned pregnancies.

Those who become pregnant need access to appropriate and quality care throughout pregnancy, childbirth and in the post-partum period. They should be supported, if they choose, to return to formal or informal school.

Put together, these actions lead to protection of girls who are already brides and those who are not, higher levels of gender equality and, in turn, just and equitable societies and more vibrant economies. No society can afford the lost opportunity, waste of talent, or personal exploitation that child marriage causes.

Nyakuti's Story

Nyakuti's parents would go to the river for fishing every day, hoping to make enough catch to sell at the local market so that they could have enough money to enroll their children to school and at the same time buy food for them. In an unlucky day, however, Nyakuti and her siblings would go to bed on empty stomachs, something they understood and bared with the situation.

When her father died, life got even harder for her family. Nyakuti's mother was left alone to fend for herself and her 10 children with no steady source of income.

"I was 12 years old when I got married to a 35 year old man. I was told that the man would take care of me, my siblings, and my mother. Due to the poverty levels, I accepted as it was too much for me to see my family suffer due to lack of food and proper medical care."

Nyakuti was aware that her mother couldn't afford to feed her, buy basic requirements and clothes for her, or pay her education, and she felt that if she rejected the prearranged marriage proposal, the family problems would still persist. Nonetheless, rather than paying the significant and the much anticipated dowry that the family had longed hoped for, which her mother could utilize to support the family, Nyakuti's new husband paid her family a single goat and two chicken as her bride price.

"I cried as I was too young to get into marriage but I had no choice. I didn't want to, I didn't understand the meaning of marriage, and I was filled with fear."

In her new role as a wife and as expected, Nyakuti dropped out of school, and instead took care of her husband as the African culture demands. She searched for menial jobs she could do to earn some money including tilling farms for the neighbours, doing laundry for the working class and babysitting. She and her husband struggled to earn enough to eat. But the greatest loss, for Nyakuti, was her freedom.

"When I was living with my mother I was free to do what I wanted to do, now in the house I was taken to, I wasn't free. I was scared because he

*denied me to do anything, and only he decided
what should be done."*

As a child bride, she also endured the horror and pain of an unwanted physical relationship. After six months, she discovered she was pregnant.

"When I got pregnant I felt so much pain because I wasn't ready to conceive at that age, I had no knowledge of how to deliver a baby. I could not afford the cost of antenatal care."

While she was still pregnant, Nyakuti's husband died and just before the funeral, her brother-in-law and successor to her late husband's land and property, married Nyakuti. She was inherited as a second wife. In her second marriage to her late husband's brother, she was often subjected to domestic violence, and as a result she lost her unborn baby. Under threat and oppression, she felt unable to seek out for help following her miscarriage.

After several years, Nyakuti eventually became pregnant for the second time. She was still pregnant when her second husband also died and Nyakuti, still only a child herself, was left alone to give birth.

"If my child could get an education, his life would be different from mine, when children are kept in school, they get educated and they reap the benefits. I would like to tell others that when you get married at an early age, things are difficult and you lose all your rights and you suffer a lot."

Tela

Tela is the oldest of five children. She was just 7 years old when her mother died and, not long after, her father was killed by a stray bullet during an armed robbery in the local town. Suddenly orphaned, Tela and her four young siblings had to leave the place where they grew up, and move in with their grandmother in a village nearby.

Her grandmother struggled to look after them, until finally she feared they couldn't survive like that for much longer. Life was unbearable for her and the children. She felt she had no choice but to arrange a marriage for Tela as a means out of the harsh life.

"I was 13 when I got married; my husband was 30 years old. It was because of extreme poverty and severe hunger. When I asked my grandmother about my education, she said the same man who will marry me will take me to school. But when I got married, that was the end of my education and my friends. I could not continue to go to school for the reason that I was supposed to take care of my husband. I was now a wife and no longer a child."

In addition to having new responsibilities as a wife, Tela also discovered she was expecting child soon after getting married. Her pregnancy was another obstacle between Tela and her education. Her schoolmates pointed and laughed at her, and the embarrassment was too much for her to bear. Instead of getting an education, Tela spent her days sweeping, washing clothes, washing dishes, collecting vegetables, collecting firewood, working in neighbouring fields, and cooking for her husband in the evenings.

"I was hurt when I discovered I was pregnant. I was too young to comprehend. I used to think that my life would improve for the better when I got married, but even the dream that I had of taking care of my young brothers and sisters turned out to be a fairy tale."

At 13, far too young to know about childbirth, or how to take care of a baby, Tela went into a terrifying and agonizing labour, which resulted in an emergency caesarean section to save her life and that of the baby.

"I'm just a child, I'm just the way you see me. And I wouldn't like anyone who is 14 to go through what I have been through. It is physical and mental torture."

Tela is still married and living in the same condition with hopes that her life will play out differently and be able to get back to where she left her studies.

Maria

Maria's mother and father both died in quick succession, leaving her and her five siblings to move in with their eldest sibling, in an impoverished fishing neighborhood.

She didn't want to get married because she was so young and loved going to school, but, when a man approached the family seeking to marry Maria, she accepted because her older sibling couldn't look after them all. If Maria were to turn down the marriage arrangement, she would have been forced to leave home and became a street beggar or a prostitute, as her family members were not able to take care of her. With nowhere else to go and no way to support herself, she agreed. She was only 14 years old.

"I hoped life would improve after getting married, and that I would help to take care of my young brothers and sisters."

But Maria and her husband had no source of income, they struggled to provide for themselves let alone support Maria's younger siblings. Her husband seldom worked, and she spent her days sweeping, cooking, and cleaning dishes. When Maria was 5 months pregnant, her husband left and never came back. He disappeared in the thin air leaving her destitute and vulnerable.

Terrified, alone, and preparing to raise a child while still a child herself, Maria was not sure of how she was going to cope. She didn't know anything about pregnancy or childbirth, all she knew is that she was far too young to be having a baby and society shunned her.

"Even after I had a child he is nowhere to be found. I was not yet at the age of becoming a mother leave alone a wife. An abandoned wife and mother."

During labour, Mary's sister helped her to deliver a healthy baby although she was dependent on other people's help to provide for herself and her baby.

"If only my mother was still alive, I would have been in school. If I were in school, my life would have been different. I may have been employed as a teacher or a nurse."

Every child has a right to quality education. Early marriage is not a solution to poverty.

CHAPTER 3
THE CHILD SOLDIER

"No child should be made to carry guns or weapon" – Mahimbo Mdoe, United Nations International Children's Emergency Fund (UNICEF) Representative in South Sudan.

Whether the recruitment is forced or voluntary, children have no role to play in wars whatsoever. Thousands of children are serving as soldiers in armed conflicts and wars around the world. These boys and girls some as young as 8 years old according to a report by United Nations International Children's Emergency Fund (UNICEF), serve in both state armed forces and non-state armed groups. These groups continue to recruit child soldiers into their camps and force them into the conflict, despite numerous commitments to stop the practice. These children are forced to fight on the front lines, participate in suicide missions, and act as spies, messengers, or lookouts. Some are abducted by armed groups and forced to steal, rape women and girls as old as their mothers, or their own mothers, sisters and aunts, engage in unlawful sexual acts such as bestiality and sometimes ordered to kill. Girls are often forced into sexual slavery and forced to marry the members of the armed groups they have been abducted into. Many are abducted or recruited by force, while others join out of desperation, with the belief that these armed groups offer best chance for survival in a conflict situation.

In South Sudan, thousands of children have been forced to join the military and other armed groups. Many children are serving in the ranks of armed forces, according to figures by United Nations International Children's Emergency Fund (UNICEF). Children who are poor, displaced from their families, have limited access to education, or live in a combat zone are more likely to be forcibly recruited. Refugee camps are breeding grounds for recruitment of children into wars.

In Tamil, children are susceptible to recruitment beginning at the early age of eleven or twelve. The rebel groups routinely visited Tamil homes to notify parents that they must give a child for the "movement." Families that resisted were harassed and threatened with murder. Parents were told that their child will be taken by force if they do not obey, that other children in the home or the parents will be taken in their place, or that the family will be forced to leave their house. The Liberation Tigers of Tamil Eelam (LTTE) that carried out the threats and the recruitment was one of the many groups that came into existence to fight for the rights of the Tamil in Sri Lanka. The conflict between the Sri Lanka's government forces and armed Tamil rebels raged for nearly 60 years. The LTTE made good of its threats: children were regularly abducted from their homes at night, or singled out up by LTTE cadres while going to school or attending religious festivals. Parents who resist the abduction of their children faced brutal LTTE revenge.

Once recruited, most children were not permitted to contact their families. The LTTE subjected them to painstaking and sometimes brutal training. They were taught to handle arms, including landmines and bombs, and were trained on military tactics. Children who made mistakes were regularly beaten and sometimes killed. The LTTE unsympathetically punished child soldiers who attempted to escape. Children who attempted to run away were beaten in front of the whole unit, a public discipline that served to deter other children who may be tempted to escape.

The recruitment of child soldiers goes against numerous human rights laws. Children who have committed crimes as soldiers are treated more leniently; crimes committed voluntarily are subject to justice under the international juvenile justice standards.

At least 65,000 children have been released from armed forces and armed groups since the last decade, according to the United Nations children's agency UNICEF. More than 200 child soldiers have been freed in South Sudan, according to UNICEF report in 2018. One hundred and twelve boys and 95 girls, some as young as 14, were freed at a special lying down of arms ceremony organized by UNICEF. The UN agency said it hoped to release around 1,000 more child soldiers in coming months and has freed more than 500 child soldiers so far by the end of 2018.

The Afghan National Police, the Afghan Local Police and other groups such as the Taliban Forces, were listed as perpetrators by the UN in 2015. Also, in the same year Child Soldiers International interviewed a 17 year old but who had signed up when he was 15 using a fake national Identity Card. During his recruitment, the doctor who conducted his medical examination ascertained his actual age.

In the Central African Republic, as many as 10,000 children were used by armed groups according to Child Soldiers International. The children were used as combatants, guards, human shields, porters, messengers, spies, cooks and or sexual purposes. In Nigeria, the terrorist group Boko Haram recruited over 2000 child soldiers in 2016 according to the UN. The group sexually exploited the girls and used them as suicide bombers.

In the year 1991 to 2002, Sierra Leone was involved in a devastating civil war, fought largely between the Revolutionary United Front (RUF) and Sierra Leone Army (SLA). The civil war garnered international attention for its blatant engagement of child soldiers and for the skyrocketing of child soldiers in Sierra Leone.

Child soldiers are children as defined under international law as persons under the age of 18 who are used for any military purpose. In the Sierra Leonean civil war, children according to a report released in 2017 by the Borgen Project a non-profit organization made up between 40 and 50 percent of the RUF's armed force and approximately 20 percent of the government's military force. In total, approximately 10,000 children were exploited and forced to be child soldiers in Sierra Leone.

As emphasized in United Nations report on the impact of armed conflict on children, children associated with armed forces or armed groups are exposed to tremendous violence, often forced to witness and commit violence, while themselves being abused, exploited, injured or even killed as a result. Their condition deprives them of their rights, often with severe physical and emotional consequences.

The UN Security Council in its 1612 resolution adopted in 2005 expressed its readiness to take appropriate sanctions against perpetrators of violence against children in armed conflict. The African Charter on the Rights and Welfare of a Child calls on State Parties to take all necessary measures to make sure that no child shall take a direct part in hostilities and refrain in particular, from recruiting any child. Also, in line with the Safe Schools Declaration adopted at the Oslo Conference on Safe Schools that define guidelines for Protecting Schools and Universities from Military Use during Armed Conflict, The AU also reaffirms the Paris Commitment and Principles on the Protection of the Children in Armed Conflict, adopted by the International Conference "Free Children from War".

Children in war benefit from the general protection on international humanitarian law as civilians or combatants. But there are also special provisions that recognize their particular vulnerability and needs in armed conflicts. The 1977 Additional Protocols to the Geneva Conventions were the first international treaties to try and protect children during war. They prohibit the recruitment and participation in hostilities of children under the age of 15. In international armed conflicts, the first additional Protocol also requires military recruitment of 15 to 18 year olds to prioritize the oldest. The Convention on the Rights of the Child also sets

the age limit to 15. An optional protocol to this
Convention lifted the age for compulsory
recruitment to 18 and called on States to raise
the minimum age for voluntary recruitment
above 15. It insisted that armed groups should
not use children under 18 in any circumstances
and called on States to criminalize such
practices.

Akot's Story

On 9 July 2011, Akot with mixed emotions of joy
and tears watched the flag of South Sudan rise
for the first time in a land that has known war
for decades, which gave him hope for a bright,
better future and peaceful and prosperous South
Sudan. In that moment, all of the pains and
misfortunes of his childhood took on a powerful
inspirational meaning.

*"I remember feeling that if I died right then, I
would do so a happy person, a warrior and a*

fulfilled person. I had lived to see my country's independence an unimaginable dream come true".
Akot attended the historic event in Juba, the capital. Men and women sat under the scorching sun with tears rolling down their cheeks. The people of South Sudan had claimed their dignity and gained their independence through a landslide "yes" vote for separation from Sudan.
"Our new flag is a symbol of conquest after a long and bloody fight, in which more people than we will ever know, died from guns and bombs, hunger and diseases. Never again the humiliation of being a second-class citizen hounded out of our homes and scattered across the five continents as refugees and Internally Displaced Persons.
His mind filled with recollections of his ordeals as a young child living in Itang refugee camp in Ethiopia. He was oblivious to the cruel realities of the violent quest for independence a free South Sudan.

"I only knew that the northerners reviled us, looked down on us and were determined on destroying us. War raged in our homelands in Sudan, and our stay in Itang stretched to four years".

Their leader, the late John Garang and first President of the Republic of South Sudan, often visited the Itang Refugee Camp and reminded them that they were part of the freedom fighters. They practiced marching drills on a daily basis, out of the sight of aid workers who were providing humanitarian assistance to the refugees inside the camp.

While at the Refugee Camp, Akot had his first experience of formal schooling. His school was in a shade under a tree. They wrote on the ground for lack of exercise books and pens. He learnt basic English and Arabic from wounded SPLA soldiers who were brought to recover in the camp. They were young boys whose education had been interrupted by the war, a war they were born and found being fought for many years.

"In May 1991 that episode of my life came to an abrupt end. Ethiopia's president, Mengistu Haile Mariam was ousted. He had supported the Sudan People's Liberation Army (SPLA) and our struggle for independence. The new regime had no interest in sheltering Sudanese refugees".

Akot cannot clearly remember how it all began. All he remembers is the exploding sound of gunfire and people running helter skater in all directions screaming. It was raining and there was a mixture of rain water and blood on the ground. He ran, first to his stepmother's house, and then to his mother's but both houses were empty.

"Amid the shooting I ran and ran as fast as my legs would carry me. I came to a river that was choked up with dead bodies. I joined those who

crossed. We marched back to Sudan. I was only thirteen years old. I was just a child like any other child in other parts of the world who were going to school, watching movies and playing in playgrounds".

Life back in Sudan was unbearable compared to the refugee camp. For food, there was little more than grass. He was alone, separated from his family and desperate to survive in the midst of violent and unforgiving chaos.

"The northern government seized the opportunity of Ethiopia's change of heart, and was bombing SPLA-controlled areas".

Worse more, the SPLA had split into rival factions that were attempting to eliminate each other. Anyone who resisted the will of either side was killed. There were no real civilians, only warriors. Everybody was armed. Everybody was at war. War was the narrative.

"You always had to protect yourself from someone. Everyone was an enemy. Everyone seemed to be enraged. No one knew who was who".

So when he found an SPLA base that agreed to take him, despite his young age, Akot had no hesitation in becoming a soldier. His duty was to clean guns and occasionally he found himself firing them. He became accustomed to the bloodshed. It was normal and a daily routine for Akot a duty he got accustomed to and enjoyed performing.

An attack in 1992 wiped out nearly everyone in the camp. The enemy had surrounded them. He fled towards the Nile River. Many soldiers drowned.

"The Nile can be treacherous. You came up for air and they popped your head".

After the fighting subsided, he went back to the SPLA base. His close friends had all been killed.

He did not have any direction after that battle which left him confused.

"I went back to Akobo to look for my mother. She had settled with my two sisters and two younger brothers in the beautiful small village of Deng Jok several miles from Akobo town. Our elder mother was also there with some of my siblings and my young stepmother".

As if death was still hounding him, one day, foreign aid workers were transporting children across the river to take part in a vaccination campaign. He and his step mother stood on the river bank, watching the motorboat speed off with about 30 children on board. His six-year-old twin sister and brother were among them. As fate would have it, they watched in horror and disbelief as the boat capsized emptying the children into the river. They quickly jumped inside the river to save the children. Unfortunately only one of the twins survived.

The rest perished as they watched helplessly and powerlessly.

"I could not take it anymore. There was no future. I dropped my gun and crossed the Nile once again into Ethiopia. Alone I walked southwards in the direction of Kenya. I never looked back. I moved at night to avoid detection. On the way, I met up with other young men. We walked for eight days without food and clean drinking water. Our feet were swollen with cuts and bruises. My toenails came off. It was painful".

He continued with his trek, surviving on stealing and using the loot to bribe his way through. He ate mangoes stolen from the villages they passed through. Hostile villagers threw stones at them. They slept in the woods or on the long grass; anywhere they could find a dry space to call a "bed" for the night.

As him and his friends got into the Ethiopian Highlands, the temperatures dropped to almost 15 degrees. It was too cold for them and all they had were torn t-shirts.

"We were scared. We didn't know the forest or the animals".

They managed to walk through Ethiopia and finally found themselves in Kenya.

The next two years were tough for Akot in the refugee camp in Kenya yet life was calm and peaceful. While there, he could manage one meal a day. A number of resettlement organizations were working towards taking Sudanese refugees to the United States and other Western countries. While there, he kept himself occupied by playing soccer and going to school while he waited for his turn which came in 1995. He was 15 years old.

Paulette's Story

"I became pregnant when I was 16. During labour, I was forced to walk for miles as the rebels were evading the Ugandan army. My son died before he was born. I was operated on to remove him, without anesthesia".

Abducted at 12, Paulette was raped and her baby died before she was lucky to escape. She spent seven years in the bush in Uganda as a child soldier, held captive by an armed group and forced to become the "wife" of a rebel commander. Her best friend was killed as she watched. Her baby died before it was born but she was lucky to escape.

"There are children in war presently, people who are forcibly taken away to fight for a cause they do not understand. That is why I stand before you here today, 12th February, during this annual commemoration to bring attention to the fate of child soldiers"

There are so many young girls in the same situation as Paulette. Fear and shame often leave these children who come back from conflict unable to talk about their experiences.

"I was told by my community to remain silent. But if survivors of child soldier remain silent, they will not get the much needed help. It is only through sharing their experiences that they can get help."

Paulette was only 12 when she was taken. Inside the camp, girls were there to be used as sex objects whenever the men wanted. Soldiers are not allowed to fall in love. If one was caught charming a girl, that was the end of his life. He was killed instantly.

"I became pregnant in the forest when I was 16. During labour, I was forced to walk for miles as the rebels were evading the Ugandan army. My son died before he was born. I was operated on to remove him, without anesthesia".

Paulette was not allowed to mourn the death of her child. Doing so would mean being killed but she never lost hope. Her health got worse after the operation and she was allowed to get treatment from Kenya. That is when a nurse helped her to escape.

"When I returned to my village, I was only given a mattress and a blanket. A blanket might keep you warm, but education is building for life."

Paulette really wanted to go back to school. Although her baby died, it gave her the opportunity to escape. She had missed seven years of her schooling but with the assistance of local non-governmental organizations, she was able to pick up her studies.

Chikwanine's Story

"I was forced literally to kill my best friend as an initiation process into the army. That is

something I will never forget, and I still fight with every single day."

Chikwanine was five years old when rebel militiamen kidnapped him from a soccer field near his school in the Democratic Republic of Congo. He had decided to stay out to play rather than follow his father's instructions to head straight home. As the fighters approached his group of friends, he was more concerned about having disobeyed his father than about what the men would do.

Chikwanine's life would quickly and irreconcilably change, however, as the militia abducted the boys and took them to its camp. There, a fighter drugged him with a mix of cocaine and gunpowder. Chikwanine was blindfolded and made to hold a gun, then told to shoot it. That his first killing mission at the age of five.

"I was forced literally to kill my best friend as an initiation process into the army. That is something I will never forget, and I still fight with every single day."

After the Rwandan genocide in 1994, millions of the country's ethnic Hutu population many of whom had participated in the campaign against the ethnic Tutsis fled into eastern Democratic Republic of Congo (DRC). Once there, Hutu extremist groups attacked Tutsis within the nation and threatened further attacks on Rwanda.

Rwanda responded by supporting a Tutsi-led rebel campaign that toppled longtime Congolese dictator Mobutu Sese Seko while also committing horrific abuses against the populace and Hutu refugees. But DRC's newly installed rebel leader-turned-president, Laurent Kabila, turned against his former Rwandan allies once in power.

In 1998, Kabila's government and Rwandan-backed rebels started warring over who would control DRC. The conflict also involved a number of regional powers backing different sides and plundering the nation's natural resources.

An estimated 30,000 children were fighting at the peak of the war, according to UNICEF. The conflict killed and injured millions, left hundreds of thousands of people homeless, and led to widespread destruction.

"When we talk about Africa, or any other part of the world, it's always talked about in headlines. Africa has a very stereotypical mention of being very violent and poor, but we forget to mention the context of the conflict and the poverty. It leads people to conclude the very stereotypical idea of what Africa is, and that's not what it is."

Chikwanine returned to the relative safety of his home after being abducted, but his family saw more suffering in the years to come. The rising instability and violence in DRC descended in the late 1990s into a civil war that killed over 5 million people and brought more attacks against Chikwanine and his family. His father, a human rights activist, was tortured and ultimately assassinated after fleeing the country, while his sisters and mother survived sexual violence.

"Sometimes, as adults, we shy away from having conversations with our own young people, but every day in the world a young person sees atrocities that are happening. It's important to start having conversations with young people, to engage them in that way if we want them to grow up to be engaged citizens in society."

Beah's Story

'Shooting became just like drinking a glass of water'

As a teenager in war-ravaged Sierra Leone, Ishmael Beah was brainwashed, drugged and forced to kill.

"We went from children who were afraid of gunshots to now children who were gunshots," says Beah who became separated from his family at just 12 years old when his town was attacked. His family was later killed in the country's vicious civil war, which lasted from 1991 to 2002. During this time rebel groups like the Revolutionary United Front (RUF) who were notorious for hacking off limbs and indoctrinating children into their battle fought government forces and their offshoots for control of the diamond rich West African state.

Hopeless for help, Beah says he wandered the countryside with a group of other children who had lost their families in similar circumstances.

They managed to avoid the roaming RUF rebels but witnessed gunfights, ransacked villages and countless dead bodies along the way.

"I saw a man carrying his son that had been shot dead, but he was trying to run with him to the hospital, there was also woman who was with her baby on her back. She'd been running away from the fighting and a bullet hit her baby and died but she didn't know."

Eventually Beah and his friends came across a rural camp they initially believed to be an army base.

They soon realized however that they had in fact stumbled upon a battalion of breakaway Sierra Leonean soldiers. The splinter groups opposed the RUF but were pursuing similarly vicious fighting tactics, including the deployment of child soldiers. Beah was taken in, given shelter and eventually trained to kill.

Violence was the order of the day. That is all he knew in his daily life. Children who refused to fight, kill or showed any weakness were ruthlessly dealt with including being killed or their hands chopped off.

"Emotions weren't allowed. For example a nine-year-old boy cried because he missed his mother and he was shot dead".

Speaking about the moment he became separated from his family, Beah recalls: *"I had gone to a talent show, I was interested in American hip-hop music, with my older brother, to another town and while away my town was attacked. I went from having an entire family in one minute to having nothing at all the next. It was very painful, I felt lost and distraught."*

Now a U.N. goodwill ambassador, a law graduate and a best-selling author, Beah is heading the fight to publicize the plight of child soldiers in Africa.

He was taken to a rehabilitation center in the Sierra Leone capital, Freetown, where he spent eight months learning about what happened to him and readjusting to life after the war.

Those who worked at the center were frequently attacked by the child soldiers who found it difficult to adapt to their new surroundings in the early days as they received rehabilitation.

"We were very angry. We were very destructive. We destroyed the center where we were staying. We burnt everything that came our way. We beat anybody that we perceived as enemy"

With time, and the patience of a care giver, Beah was eventually able to reconnect to his lost childhood and remember the person he once was.

*Every Child has a right to special
protection and help.*

CHAPTER 4
THE CAMP WOMAN

To the world they are known as refugees. They are nameless, faceless and sometimes stateless. But each of them has a story to tell of their lives, who they lost, and how they got there. Fleeing from devastating conflict in various parts of the world, today they are rebuilding their lives, one day at a time, (despite the harsh conditions in refugee camps. Their lives condemned there with no hopes of ever leaving).

Millions of people have fled civil wars with tones of thousands living in refugee camps. Adapting to a new life after fleeing the trauma of war is incredibly difficult. Most refugee families live in poverty. They have difficulties finding employment and education opportunities. Post-traumatic symptoms, such as anxiety and depression, are common. Many hope for asylum in western countries to save themselves from the harsh conditions of camp life.

The refugee crisis in the world is getting worse. Refugee camps are cramped, and thousands of people are living in extreme poverty, without access to basic needs like electricity and clean water. Violence against women is escalating and becoming the new normal in camps across the world.

According to a UNHCR report, 68.5 million people were forcibly displaced worldwide as a result of persecution, conflict, violence or human rights violations. In the Central African Republic, nearly one million men, women and children fled their homes in desperation, seeking refuge in mosques and churches, as well as neighbouring countries such as the Democratic Republic of Congo, Chad and the Republic of Congo.

In the ongoing conflict and violence in Syria, Iraq and other parts of the world is causing large scale displacement and refuges seeking safety beyond the immediate region. The lack of an increased number of legal pathways leaves so many people fleeing persecution with few choices, including trying to reunite with families in Europe. This has led to millions of people to take their chances on board unseaworthy boats and dinghies in a desperate effort to reach Greece, Italy and Spain en-route to Europe.

South Sudan is the world's fastest growing refugee crisis. Since December 2003, brutal conflict in South Sudan has claimed thousands of lives and driven 3.3 million people from their homes. While an estimated 1.9 million people remain displaced inside the country, 1.4 million have fled as refugees to neighbouring countries in a frantic bid to reach safety. Uganda currently hosts the most South Sudanese refugees having taken in more than 1 million people.

The life of refugee women is a burden since they have to take the responsibility of raising their families amidst many challenges. Food, one of the basic needs is inadequate as the supply is not predictable and most of the time the family has to adopt skipping meals to make ends meet. In health issues, the woman has to take charge to correct the situation. Most of these women are widows, single parents either divorced or separated during the war as each sought for safety. While gang raping and abduction remains a painful ordeal for a refugee woman, most of the traditional practices have preference towards a boy child rather than a girl child, for instance during food distributions days, only girls are out of school to collect the family rations from the distribution centers. This is because issues of food is taken to be a woman's responsibility and is seen as a requirement and an obligation for a traditional woman. Commercial sex and illicit beer brewing are among some of the income generating activities within the camp.

Girls and women in refugee camps are particularly vulnerable because of their age and gender. Girls suspend their studies more often than boys and many have to marry young in order to support their families. Sexual violence also typically becomes more pronounced in a time of crisis and in such a setting.

In times of crisis women bear the brunt. Although all refugees are marginalized, women are particularly vulnerable to exploitation and physical sexual harm, pregnant women and those with small children are uniquely vulnerable. All over refugee camps, there are extensive reports of gender-based violence. For refugee women and children living in camps, violence has become a normalized part of their lives. Street harassment and rape within the camps are also issues. Girls are told it is inappropriate for them to voice anything publicly or to scream, even when they are in danger. In addition, forced and child marriage is common in refugee camps. Some families see marrying off their young daughters as a chance to keep their daughters safe, to protect family honor, and to get out of poverty given their limited economic options. They do not see it as a form of violence.

Women are affected the most by poor access to sanitation and water. Washing clothes for large families in a refugee camp laundry is an unfeasible task. In some cases women deliberately do not drink water so that they could avoid going to the deplorable and pathetic toilets. In some cases six toilets in a camp of over 600.

Women also in camps do not want to be intimate with their partners for fear of getting pregnant and for the lack of provision of good maternity care.

In the midst of all the chaos and despite high levels of poverty, risk, trauma, and violence, which disproportionately fall on women, it is women who are at the forefront of long-term efforts to build the community, create sustainable change, protect and extend human rights. Women in refugee camps work tirelessly to empower themselves as well as working to change the norms around violence, create safe spaces for women and empower women and girls to understand and demand their rights. Further, UN Women among other NGOs support economic and social rehabilitation to vulnerable women, survivors of conflict and sexual gender-based violence.

It took the United Nations only 13 years to adopt the Convention on the Elimination of Discrimination Against Women (CEDAW) yet still discrimination continues including places like refugee camps. Rule of law promotes good governance-transparent, accountable institutions, equal access to justice and respect for human rights and so is an essential ingredient to sustainable development. A core principle of the rule of law is equality. We are all equal in the eyes of the law, equally protected by the law and equally accountable to it. The rule of law, properly applied, is the best antidote for gender inequality.

Women groups are at the vanguard of changing attitudes and behaviors within the camps. In addition to workshops they provide to women and girls basic needs such as clean drinking water, sanitary supplies and clothes. Various nongovernmental organizations also work with men and boys to help change norms about violence and women's rights. For instance, Palestinian Women's Humanitarian

Organization (PWHO)has been for a long time engaging men to do outreach and educate more men about women's rights and women's unique needs, including the importance of sexual and reproductive health.

Organizations such as Global Fund for Women's grantee partners, UN Women, UNFPA are also working on a national and international scale

Women's groups are filling vital gaps in order to meet the needs of refugees in the camps, and driving long-term change around women's human rights.

There is little resources to take care of women's and children's most immediate needs, let alone to expand maternal and new-born healthcare, increase access to contraception, support women's income-generating projects, or oppose the increasing culture of violence against women and children. Without continued efforts on these essential facets of women's rights, the future for refugee women and children in the camps is bleak.

While there are numerous organizations providing psychological support and emergency relief to children in particular, proving broader empowerment programs for women is essential to shift power and support real and sustained change within the refugee camps.

The Women at the Gado Refugee Camp

Hawa, 23, was eight months expectant with a child when her husband was killed in the fighting in the Central African Republic. Her father and brother were also killed and her mother disappeared, leaving her alone with no support and no one to turn to. She fled into Cameroon and became a refugee at the Gado Refugee Camp, where she gave birth to a healthy bouncing baby boy.

Being a widow and a refugee did not discourage her from engaging in economic activity within the camp in order to feed herself and her son. Hawa carries her son to the market everyday as her neighbour helped push a cart full of bags of cassava flour, dried fish and nuts to sell at the camp's marketplace.

"When I arrived I didn't have anyone. I received counseling from UN Women staff. They sensitized and trained me on how to do a business plan at the camp."

Ardo Djibo Fadimatou 64 lost 8 of her 15 children during the armed conflict and she does not know the whereabouts of her husband whether he is still alive or dead. She speaks for the over 12,000 women in the Gado refugee camp as their elected President and leads meetings in UN Women's Social Cohesion Space. She herself is a refugee in the camp.

"The major problem I face as a female leader is to convince parents to send their children to regular schools. Most parents prefer their children to stay at home and learn the Koran. Women need to be educated, to have income-generating activities and be able to contribute to social cohesion here at the camp."

Yaya Dia Adama escaped Central African to the Gado Refugee Camp with her five children. A tailor by profession she was able to make a living using the sewing machines at the UN Women multipurpose centre. She also trained three other women to make clothes, and together the women make dresses to sell in the market.

"Each day I am able to earn 1000 to 2000 francs a day [USD 1.75-3.50]. This has helped me to provide for my children."

Selina Hamadou, 22, also lives in the refugee camp and works as a food vendor.

"UN Women trained me on a business plan, provided me with financial assistance, which I reinvested in my restaurant at the roadside. I started saving 5,000 francs [USD 8.50] a day and when I had 200,000 francs (USD 350), I decided to start building my own house."

The Story of the Women in Kakuma Refugee Camp

Jane was a happily married wife and mother whose daily routine revolved around caring for her husband and three children. This peaceful life disintegrated into a nightmare since the appearance of her brother into her matrimonial house. His brother camped on her doorstep following the family emissary sent to get her back from her husband's house for a marriage to another man who apparently was the higher bidder in Southern Sudan, who was able to provide the 50 heads of cattle that her family demanded as bride price also known as dowry. Her husband had fled to safety on a nearby town while Jane lived in constant fear of being kidnapped and smuggled back to Southern Sudan to her new proposed suitor ignoring the fact that she was already married with children. Enraged by her refusal to return, Jane's brother threatened to take away the children instead. He knew only too well that if he abducted her children including her breastfeeding infant, she would be forced to follow.

Jane's case is one of many at Kakuma refugee camp in Northern Kenya where the kidnapping of women and children constitute the majority of cases of gender violence. Like other women, she is a victim of the Dinka and Nuer of South Sudan custom of forced marriage. Jane and her husband wedded in Southern Sudan while fleeing the war. A refugee, he was not capable to complete payment of the bridal dowry owed to her family.

*Gender equality is an empowerment
tool.*

CHAPTER 5
THE UNNECESSARY RITE

"My mother circumcised me, married me off to a 60 year old man"-Unknown.

Hanna was only seven at the time when her mother and grandmother wanted her genitals sliced off as part of fulfilling traditions. However she was lucky to be saved by her aunt after a British charity in the area, launched an awareness program on the consequences of female circumcision, a tradition widely practiced throughout parts of Africa and the Middle East.

There is no precise statistics of how many women and girls have been subjected to the procedure but it is projected that over two million procedures are performed every year. Amnesty International estimates that over 130 million women worldwide have undergone female genital mutilation. According to a 2016 UNICEF report, dubbed Female Genital Mutilation/Cutting: A Global Concern. More than 200 million girls and women alive today have been cut majority in Africa, The Middle East and Asia where Female Genital Mutilation is concentrated. In Ethiopia, 70 to 80 per cent of women are circumcised. In Kenya, the practice has been outlawed since 2001, yet in spite of the ban, a public health survey in 2009 found that 27% of women had been subjected to Female Genital Mutilation. Among some ethnic groups, such as the Somalis, (98%) and Maasai (73%).A second set of laws passed in 2011 made it illegal to promote or facilitate what used to be known as female circumcision, and stiffened penalties. But changing the law was easier than changing the practice.

The Wagogo community in Tanzania is abandoning the traditional circumcision of girls and instead adopting an alternative harmless passage to womanhood. Although Female Genital Mutilation is against the law in Tanzania, many girls are still forced to secretly go through the ritual, with the justification of maintaining cultural or religious practices.

Also happening in Australia, Female Genital Mutilation is at an estimated 83,000 women and girls having been affected, and as many as 1,100 children a year are at risk of being forced to endure the practice.

Female Genital Mutilation is not a culture, it is violence and torture. It is a human rights abuse, it is child abuse and it is sexual abuse. It cannot be reversed once it has been done. It includes procedures that deliberately alter or cause injury to the female genital organs for non-medical reasons. The procedure has no health benefits for girls and women. It can cause severe bleeding and problems during urination and later cysts, infections, as well as complications during childbirth and greater risk of neonatal deaths. It is carried out on young girls between infancy and age 18.

Female Genital Mutilation has been prohibited in Burkina Faso since 1996, making it one of the first African countries to outlaw the gruesome practice. According to the UN's children's agency, UNICEF, three-quarters of women aged 15-49 have undergone the procedure while the vast majority of people oppose **Female Genital Mutilation.** However, according to the report, there are fears that cutters and families who strongly believe in the practice are increasingly crossing the border with Mali, where there is no law on Female Genital Mutilation, and Ivory Coast, where the law is not enforced as robustly. To avoid detection, those practicing Female

Genital Mutilation are also moving away from group ceremonies to individual cutting in private. There are many other examples of cultural practices that breach the internationally protected rights of women. In Afghanistan, the Taliban, who have recently fought their way to power, prohibited women from attending school or working outside the home. Women are not even permitted to leave the house unless in the company of a male relative.

In China, female infanticide is practiced; in India, brides may be burned to death if the dowry they bring to the marriage is too small; in the West Bank and Gaza, unmarried women suspected of bringing dishonor to their families by losing their virginity may be killed while is some parts of Kenya, widowed women are required to "sleep" with their husbands corpse before burial in order to fulfill a traditional rite.

Although the focus is on women's rights, there are just as many instances of governmental norms justified by culture or religion that violate the rights of men, as well. For example, many countries have ignored the right to freedom of thought, conscience, and religion.

In some African context, Female Genital Mutilation (FGM) is considered as an indispensable part of bringing up a girl, and a way to get her ready for adulthood and marriage. It is motivated by beliefs about what is considered acceptable sexual behaviors. It aims to ensure pre-marital virginity and marital fidelity. In many communities, it is believed to reduce a woman's libido and therefore believed to help her resist extramarital affairs.

In every society where it is practiced, Female Genital Mutilation is a manifestation of deeply entrenched gender inequality. It persists for many reasons. In some societies, for example, it is considered a rite of passage. In others, it is seen as a prerequisite for marriage. In some communities, whether Christian, Jewish, Muslim – the practice may even be attributed to religious beliefs.

Because Female Genital Mutilation may be considered an important part of a culture or identity, it may not be easy for families to decide against having their daughters undergo the practice. People who refuse the practice may face condemnation or exclusion from the society, and their daughters are sometimes considered ineligible for marriage. As a result, even parents who do not want their daughters to undergo Female Genital Mutilation may feel bound to take part in the practice.

Female Genital Mutilation has been universally condemned by the World Health Organization in a resolution which was passed in 2013, and there are ongoing global campaigns aimed at stopping the practice. It is recognized internationally as a violation of the human rights of girls and women. It reflects deep-rooted inequality between the sexes, and constitutes an extreme form of discrimination against women. The practice also violates a person's rights to health, security and physical integrity, the right to be free from torture and cruel, inhumane or degrading treatment, and the right to life when the procedure results in death.

In 2012, the United Nations General Assembly adopted a resolution on the elimination of female genital mutilation in an aim to intensify global efforts against the vice. The resolution intensified the need for states to develop long term and strategic vision, where punitive measures are complemented with awareness-raising, educational activities and the protection of women and girls. The resolution also calls on the international community to support an end to female genital mutilation through ensuring the allocation of financial resources, as well as by taking into account the protection and promotion of the rights of women and girls in all program and activities.

The African Union has adopted legally binding instruments that promote the prohibition of traditional practices that are prejudicial to the health and welfare of young girls and women. Among others, the African Charter on the Rights and Welfare of the Child Article 21 obligates State parties to eliminate harmful social and cultural practices, such as Female Genital Mutilation, that affect the welfare, dignity, normal growth and development of the child.

Collective abandonment, in which a whole community chooses to no longer engage in Female Genital Mutilation, is an effective way to end the practice. It ensures that no single girl or family will be disadvantaged by the decision.

Many experts hold that Female Genital Mutilation will only end through collective abandonment.

The decision to collectively abandon Female Genital Mutilation requires a process in which communities are educated about Female Genital Mutilation, and then discuss, reflect and reach a consensus on the issue. The health and human rights aspects of Female Genital Mutilation should feature prominently in these dialogues, and local grassroots organizations should play an important role in raising awareness and educating communities.

When communities choose to abandon the practice, they often participate in a collective public declaration to keep their girls uncut. Such as signing and circulating a public statement or hosting festivities to celebrate the decision. Neighboring communities are often invited to these events so they can see the successful process of abandonment, helping to build momentum for collective abandonment elsewhere.

In 2008, UNFPA and UNICEF established a Joint Program on Female Genital Mutilation, a global program to step up abandonment of Female Genital Mutilation and to give care for its consequences. This program works at the community, national, regional and global levels to increase awareness of the harms caused by Female Genital Mutilation and to empower communities, men, women and girls to make the choice to abandon it.

Presently in its third phase of implementation, the Joint Program has helped more than 3.2 million girls and women obtain shelter against Female Genital Mutilation and specialized care services. Some 31.6 million people in more than 21,700 communities in 15 countries with high Female Genital Mutilation prevalence have made public declarations to abandon the harmful practice.

UNFPA also helps support health services to prevent Female Genital Mutilation and to treat complications caused. The UN agency also works in partnerships with civil society organizations on the health and human rights aspects of the practice.

The Fund works with religious and traditional leaders to de-link Female Genital Mutilation from religion and to generate support for abandonment.

Many countries have passed laws outlawing Female Genital Mutilation in 2015, including Nigeria and The Gambia had developed national policies to achieve its abandonment.

Farida's Story

Farida was only 20 years old married with four children. Born in 1993 and attended primary school briefly before she was forcefully married off by her parents to a 60 year old man.

"It was 3am in the morning of 2003. Confused, I was grabbed by three old women. They Shook me to consciousness and under the thick cover of darkness, whisked me off to some secluded location. I was confused and unaware of what was going on. I was panic stricken and afraid".

She screamed, but her mother held her mouth firm and asked her to oblige. She tried to run away but I was easily over powered due to her small body. What seemed like an everlasting journey, full of anguish and turmoil, she was taken into a poorly-lit scraggly hut handed over to a mean looking old woman. She grinned like a witch and her eyes were cold and her hands were very course like a crocodile skin.

"Tossing me around, she ordered that the other woman hold me tight on the floor and undressed me. And right there, other old women held me

down, my own mother included. They stripped me naked and ordered that I spread my legs. I refused and started screaming to no avail of sympathy".

Farida was too young to comprehend the scale of the whole matter.

"A dirty piece of cloth was stuffed into my mouth and I was firmly held down while my legs forcefully pulled apart. I could feel an attempt to cut through my genitals. I heard it again, and I passed out. I came to consciousness hours later and it was daytime".

Farida had been initiated to womanhood following traditions and ready for marriage; her genitals had been cut off and stitched up. Stitched like a torn piece of cloth joined together. Stitched with a thorn, yes a sharp hard thorn plucked from a thorn tree. She had bled profusely. Her mother and the other women forced her swallow bitter concoctions of local herbs to manage the excruciating pain she was experiencing.

"It was hell on earth. I couldn't pass urine. After what seemed like forever, the wound healed. I was now the latest victim of an unwanted rite- Female Genital Mutilation. A tradition that continues to exists abated by those in authority".

A year later, in 2004, Farida's parents planned a forced marriage for her. Her elder sisters were part of the arrangement. A man, well over 60 years of age was introduced to her as her groom. Farida in dire shock while balancing tears almost collapsed. Her school had come to a halt. Her future was dark. It was gloom and the thought of it infuriated her more.

She excused herself for a short call. But once outside, she fled to the chief's camp whereby she met with the chief and narrated her entire ordeal to him. Well, she was wrong. Naively wrong.

That was the mistake of her life. She had jumped out of the frying pan to the fire.

The Chief pretended to sympathize with her and locked her up in a dark room on the pretence that he was hiding her from her parents. Surprisingly her parents and the entire clan who were organizing the marriage showed up at the Chief's camp with the bride groom.

"It later turned out that the Chief sold me out. He alerted my people to come for me."

Sheep, chicken and goats were exchanged as Farida bride price and at the tender age of 11, Farida was a wife to a 60 year old man already married to three other wives. Farida was an additional fourth wife. To him she wasn't an equal married partner to their marriage. She was only there to make babies.

She gave birth to 5 children, 2 of whom died due to ill health and malnutrition.

In 2009, she managed to escape from her marital home and with the help of the Catholic Church was enrolled for rehabilitation and adult education school. Farida is now looking forward to be a nurse.

The Story of Nana

"I remember screaming in pain"

When Nana was 9 years old, she was taken on holiday by her mother and another elder woman to the bush of Gambia where she was held down by her mother while an old lady took a blunt, rusty old knife and cut off her clitoris and labia. I remember screaming in agony as I was cut, inch by inch. The trauma of that experience lives with her to this day.

"Chronic pain, pelvic infections, development of cysts, abscesses and genital ulcers, excessive scar tissue formation, infection of the reproductive system, decreased sexual enjoyment and post-

traumatic stress disorder are just some of the long term effects of Female Genital Mutilation"

When her and her family moved to Australia as a 13 year old in 2001, she realized that the practice is known as Female Genital Mutilation. She was very angry that she was subjected to this unnecessary act of violence in the name of tradition.

"I have had a precious part of my body removed that cannot be replaced"

She bled for weeks constantly battling infections and pelvic pains but was fortunate to survive to tell her story. Most of which do not get the chance to live through the ordeal to tell. Many die from this brutal custom. Although the practice has existed for generations, she hopes that it will one day stop and those who practice to get a clear visual on how it really affects one, not physically but also mentally.

*Female Genital Mutilation is a
human right violation*

CHAPTER 6
THE INHERITED WIFE

The African culture is rich and deep-rooted. Many communities still believe that if you do not follow culture strictly, you would perish. For instance throughout sub-Saharan Africa, the custom of widow cleansing and wife inheritance dictates that when a man dies, his wife and children are taken, in simple terms inherited by a surviving brother of her late husband. Widely practiced across the entire continent, it is a tradition where a widow gets inherited by relatives of her late husband. This gives the widow no choice of choosing a partner of her choice upon the death of her husband. Wikipedia defines widow inheritance as a cultural and social practice in which a widow is obligated to get married to a male family member of her late husband, most often his brother. It is also known as bride inheritance and this most often happens after a ritual known as sexual cleansing.

India has come a long way, when women were burnt alive, either willingly or through the use of force or coercion, over their husband's funeral pyre- a heap of combustible material, especially one for burning a corpse as part of a funeral ceremony. However widows in India still face continual discrimination and abuse, including sexual abuse, forced labour and impoverishment and as such there is an urgent need to raise awareness to right the wrongs committed against widows.

Widow's rights are women's rights and are human rights as well. Ignoring the wants and concerns of widows around the world is ignoring a violation of the basic human rights of the most neglected of women. When widows are denied the right to access, own, control or inherit property and the land they live on, it is a violation of their rights. When these women and their children are evicted from their homes because their husbands have died for the reason that they have refused to be inherited, it is a violation of their rights.

There has been criticism by many, who say it can be done away with, especially in this era of HIV/AIDS. In a report by Human Rights Watch in 2006, researchers observed that even when widows publicly declared their HIV-positive status, they were still inherited. Stephen Buckely, former dean at the Poynter Institute of Media studies in Florida, in his writing in The Washington Post in 1997, decried the deceptive nature of the practice, which always works to a man's advantage.

Widows who are forced into exploitative and risky sex work in order to support themselves and their families are bearing a burden that is unfair and unjust. And enduring traditional practices directed at widows, which are inhumane and degrading, is a serious violation of their human rights.

According to AllAfrica.com, "Wife inheritance has different forms and functions in different parts of the world and cultures, serving as a societal protection for and control over, the widow and her children."

In fact, wife inheritance also known as widow inheritance was practiced in the prehistoric and biblical times in the form of levirate marriage. In 1998, a research by FAO in Ghana showed that women's right to use to land was mainly through their husbands. It is a custom that when the husband dies, and if the wife is either childless or has daughters only from the marriage, then these widows are more likely than not to lose all rights to the property. More than often, the husband's family shuns any responsibility of taking care of the widow and her children. Numerous reports have shown that widow inheritance then becomes a major obstacle to family, food, security.

Promotion of gender equality to put to an end to the challenges faced by widows is a task that should be undertaken by all. For as long as daughters face discrimination and are devalued – especially in the context of poor families with limited choices – simply outlawing harmful practices against widows will not solve the problem. Practices and behaviors will only change when girls' and women's rights are respected and upheld.

There is an urgent need to support women's empowerment programs and to end violence against women. Several organizations advocates for legislative reforms and the enforcement of laws to promote and protect women's rights, including widows' rights, right to reproductive health choices and informed consent.

Poverty, illiteracy and ignorance of the law of inheritance relegate widows from time to time to unspeakable suffering, and when the system of powers that should be on their defense collude with greedy family members to defraud them, this backpedals any optimism of justice for such women.

In some cases, the women practice it willingly due to ignorance of the many risks involved in the practice. At just 28 years of age, Netari has been inherited three times and she says she will not turn down a forth suitor should the tradition that considers any woman who refuses to be inherited an outcast.

Though the practice of widow cleansing and widow inheritance is internationally considered a discrimination suffered by women by virtue of their gender, to those that practice consider it to be harmless cultural rite that protects the women from societal dangers.

In addressing the issue, there have been several international and local initiatives. The United Nations Charter and the Women's Convention on the elimination of all Forms of Discrimination against Women (CEDAW), The African Union Solemn Declaration on Gender Equality and the SADC Gender and Development Protocol, have been put in place to counter the practice related to widow cleansing and inheritance of widows. It is a collective responsibility, as the international community, leaders, and women and men to safeguard the rights and dignity of widows.

Despite these international and local efforts, there are still limitations to those initiatives. The lack of participation of women in key processes such as policy formulation and implementation, the lack of domestication of international treaties continue to hamper the process.

Edward Saguti, in his thesis Alternative Rituals of Widow Cleansing in Relation to Women's Sexual Rights in Zambia explored alternative rituals of widow cleansing in relation to women's sexual rights in Zambia. According to him, widow inheritance is a cultural practice in Zambia monitored by elders. While widowers are also expected to go through sexual cleansing, the manner in which the ritual is performed is so patriarchal and favors the men more than the women. Men are advantaged because of the polygamous culture practiced in many communities, wherein they are allowed to have more than one wife. In case of the death of a wife a man can cleanse himself with the other wife or wives, and if not in polygamous marriage, he can easily get another wife. Widows on the other hand cannot remarry, but are expected to be cleansed and inherited.

Shukri's Story

"The widow must then have sexual intercourse after the death of her husband with men unknown to her to be cleansed. These men are people of little or no worth in the community, and are paid to do the job".

Shukri's nightmare began when her husband died in 2003, a situation that put her through a vicious dispute with her in laws.

As soon as a woman is widowed, among the Suba community in the Western part of Kenya, she is considered "unclean". A ceremony must, therefore, be held to cleanse the widow. The ritual includes disposing of the man's personal articles such as clothes, and acts as a precursor to the woman being inherited by another man.

"The widow must then have sexual intercourse with men to be cleansed. These men are people of

little or no worth in the community, and are paid to do the job".

It is a ritual that has contributed to the spread of HIV in the region, a practice that Shukri, a teacher was vehemently opposed to.

"If you offer refreshments to a male visitor in your own house, someone else has to do it on your behalf. If the visitor leaves his shirt or coat in the house, he is forced to live with you. It is a primitive custom"

A widow is not allowed to freely interact with men. When such a woman visits the neighbors, she is not allowed to sit on a chair. Instead, she is to sit on the floor adding that one is not allowed to serve food to a man.

"If a man is genuinely interested in you and who desires to marry you after your husband's death, he must wait until you have gone through the process of cleansing. I wanted nothing to do with it"

Her in-laws were however adamant that she goes through the cleansing ritual and a cleansing ceremony was organized behind her back by her father-in-law. Upon discovering the plot, she made it clear that she would not go through the ritual.

As a result, she was forced to leave her matrimonial home. Feeling dishonored, she left her home together with her two children and settled in a different town nearby. Her problems were far from over.

Her husband was a government employee and had some savings in the bank and also had a life insurance. Immediately after his death, my sister in law took all his documents. Without these documents, Shukri could not claim her late husband's property, and her father in-law seized the moment to try and disinherit her, through forgery.

Somehow, her late husband's family managed to forge my death certificate luckily the plan did not go through when the Sacco suspected forgery and notified Shukri. It took her intervention to prevent her father-in-law from being prosecuted for a criminal offence in forgery, since he was the one that presented the fake documents.

"I could not involve the area chief, who I suspected was colluding with my late husband's family to defraud me. He was the one who had certified my death, knowing too well that I was alive"

Fortunately for her, the District Officer at that time together with other elders prevailed upon her late husband's family to hand over her property. The tug of war between her and her family has since ended.

Mary's Story

"My in-laws told me that I was not one of them. They said that since their son and brother was no more, I could not stay in the home anymore"

Mary 50 from Kenya, at the time was widowed in 2007 leaving her with three children, then four, five and one.

Her tribulations began immediately her husband died. She was thrown out of the family home hardly six months after losing her husband.

Immediately after the burial of her husband, she was called before a meeting and asked to choose from her husband's brothers who would be her husband. Mary refused and stormed out of the family meeting. That is when her tribulations began

"My in-laws told me that I was not one of them. They said that since their son and brother was no more, I could not stay in the home anymore"

Whereas this added onto her grief, it also emboldened her to fight for her rightful share of the family's land. At first, she swore not to leave her husband's home, but when her late husband's relatives pulled down her house, her persistence caved in, and she was forced to leave.

"I was still breastfeeding my youngest son at the time. Thankfully, my brother rented a small house for us at the shopping centre, where I lived" Neglected and shunned by the very people who had always been supportive when her husband was alive, life has not been kind to Mary and her young family. She works as a casual labourer in rice paddies while doing odd jobs to take care after her young family.

Everyone has a right to enter into marriage with the free and full consent of the intending spouse.

CHAPTER 7
THE EVILS OF ELECTION

Democratic systems in Africa have seen many countries conducting peaceful and fair elections. It has been adopted by all and sundry. It has conferred the power to rule to the people. A fundamental bed rock of democracy is the voting of political leaders through a transparent and fair electoral process.

The process gives the electorate the sole right and confidence to elect their favorite political leaders. It is a primary component in the transition from totalitarian and authoritarian to democratic ruling power. However, electoral process in the African continent have more that often been characterized by violence at various stages, from pre-election, during elections and post elections. This electoral process which gives rights to the people to govern themselves has been challenges by the threats to security, peace and development. Experiences from around the world, for example in Afghanistan and Colombia, demonstrate that elections can degenerate into violence and bloodshed. Violent elections deter people from exercising their political rights and risk undermining the legality of democratic institutions.

Across Africa, very violent elections have occurred with disputed presidential elections outcome resulting into post-election violence in Ethiopia 2005, Nigeria 2007, Zimbabwe 2008, Ivory Coast 2010 and more recently Gabon in 2016, among others. Children are exposed to utter brutality, witnesses to violence or even death of their families or neighbors most of which were never quick or painless. With use of various weapons from machetes to fire arms fired without thought or any direction. Ever since the end of the Cold War, developing countries all over the world have experienced an increase in election violence. From inter-communal skirmishing in Kenya and India, to intra-ethnic hostility in Burundi and Sri Lanka, to partisan violence in Bangladesh and Zimbabwe, it is presently obvious that elections serve as critical focal points about which atrocious conflict can happen. Existing comparative reports on election violence has clearly shown that even though there are unprompted elements to such conflicts, electoral clashes typically erupt from calculated leader's well planned ideologies. A new study on electoral violence has begun to consider not only the profits but also the costs of election violence. Consequently it is safe to state that over the years, electoral conflict has become a dedicated area of research and policy analysis,

124

with scholars and practitioners alike investigating such violence in sub-Saharan Africa, South and Southeast Asia, Latin America, and Eastern Europe.

The United Nations Development Program (UNDP) defines electoral violence also known as electoral conflict as: "acts or threats of coercion, or physical harm perpetrated to affect an electoral process or that arise in the context of electoral competition." Fischer in his book Electoral Conflict and Violence defines electoral violence as "any random or organized act that seeks to determine, delay, or otherwise influence an electoral process through threat, verbal intimidation, hate speech, disinformation, physical assault, forced 'protection,' blackmail, destruction of property, or assassination.

The effects of electoral violence can cause lasting physical, mental and emotional harm include behavioral and emotional symptoms like fear, aggression, irregular sleep patterns, disturbed play, learning general Post Traumatic Stress Disorders.

Electoral violence in an African election can be seen manifested in various forms of human rights violations such as physical assaults, arson, rape, murder. It is caused by unemployment and poverty and most of the time it gives room for the unemployed majority to be manipulated to perpetuate all forms of electoral violence. Poverty is the state of being extremely poor. It is a situation whereby the individual is not able to meet the basic necessity of life. A person exposed to these hardships is more likely to engage in electoral violence. When economic hardship becomes too unbearable, the propensity for violence increases.

Also, electoral violence can be attributed to the culture of impunity, weak governance and corruption. Corruption can set the stage for structural violence, weak governance; political exclusion and corruption; inequitable sharing of resources makes people feel desperate enough to seek any means of revenge against political authority including violence. Small arms proliferation in African countries is on the increase. Possession of arms leads to the perpetuation of violent conflict and the creation of new cycles of violence and crime.

Electoral violence leads to political instability. It is a threat to building a strong, efficient and visible democratic society. It leads to anti-human acts which include violation of human rights, issues of gender equality, cultural rights. These adversely affect the human security and social development of Africa.

When deadly electoral violence occurs, the social, economic and political consequences go beyond state boundaries. This was true in Lesotho (1998), Nigeria (1999, 2003, 2007, and 2011),

Kenya (2007), Zimbabwe (2008), Côte d'Ivoire (2010) and the Democratic Republic of the Congo (2011). In Kenya, for instance, during the 2007/2008 post-election violence that claimed over 1000 innocent souls, transportation systems from the port of Mombasa to Uganda, Rwanda and beyond was hampered. The effects of the violence was felt far and beyond.

The Story of Elizabeth

"I was only 17 years old and a high school student when the Kenya2007/2008 post-election violence broke out. I ended up being ganged raped"

It was in December 31st 2007 when Elizabeth had visited her step mother in a slum in Nairobi to celebrate the New Year when hell broke loose.

On her way to her elder sister's house within the same estate, she met with a group of about 30 youths estimated to be between the age of 14-35 from a different ethnic community. They were armed with crude weapons supposedly protesting against a stolen election. They talked to her in their language of which she could not understand. Upon realizing that she could not speak their language, they hit her with a blunt object and she fainted.

"I woke up the following day, beside the road completely naked and bleeding profusely".

A Good Samaritan called for an ambulance and she was loaded into a track, driven to hospital for medical care. She stayed in hospital for three days before she could be discharged.

The psychological torture and emotional pain she went through was immeasurable. Three weeks later, she realized that she was pregnant.

"My friends and relatives advised me to abort the baby to allow me continue with my education"

Elizabeth however chose to keep the pregnancy to term and on 30th August, 2008 she gave birth to a baby girl.

Elizabeth is now a gender activist creating awareness about sexual violence.

Fatuma's Story

"I just sit and wait to die"

Fatuma was 17 when she was gang-raped at their home in Nairobi by three men who accused her family of hiding men from the 'enemy" tribe. She stopped going to school after the rape. Fatuma said her neighbours stigmatized her son because he was born from rape.

Fatuma was hiding in her house in the sprawling slum of Kibera in Nairobi when the door was knocked open. Fearing for her life, she ran to hide under the bed. A gang of 20 men stormed into the house and dragged her and the other girls outside. She was in the house with 5 of her neighbours, girls aged 5-25.

"I could feel the pain of the dirty men, both old and young tear my pant". I was raped in turns until I blacked out. I don't know... when I gained consciousness, I found myself in a ditch. I dragged myself out of the ditch where the police rescued and took me to the rescue center until when the violence ended".

After three months of missing her monthly period, and during the regular school term pregnancy checkup on all the girls, she tested positive for pregnancy and was subsequently expelled from school as pregnant girls are not allowed in school.

Fatuma now hawks vegetables to take care of herself and her daughter since her mother could not afford to take her back school and at the same time raise her daughter.

*A peaceful and democratic election is
an obligation for all participating
parties.*

CHAPTER 8
THE FORCED TERRORIST

"No single nation, institution, or organization can defeat terrorism in Africa or anywhere else"-United Nations Secretary General António Guterres.

Many people join terrorist organizations for various reasons. Some join for economic benefits, others for religious reasons while others are forcibly recruited. According to research conducted in Somalia by the European Institute of Peace, 27% of the respondents joined Al Shabaab for economic reasons, 15% mentioned religious reasons and 13% were forced to join. Employment opportunities and skill trainings are solutions to delivering economic opportunities to susceptible youth groups but that alone would is not enough to stop young people from joining extremist groups. With an example of Somalia, the root causes included foreign involvement, most notably of non-Muslim countries. This again shows that the root causes of terrorism are diverse and very complex. As such there is no single typology to describe it. However, as mentioned earlier, the main causes of radicalization and terrorism are more often than not socio-economic. The absence of social, political and economic opportunities are a huge problem in many of the countries in which terrorist groups are active. The lack of social, political and economic opportunities can lead to alienation, frustrations, humiliation and hopelessness. Additionally, conflicts and failed states create safe havens for extremist groups allowing groups such as ISIS and Al Shabaab to thrive and maintain their relevance.

Religion, Islam in particular is used by recruiters, foreign fighters and extremists to recruit fight and justify their actions. So yes, religion plays an important role. A study conducted by Dr Anneli Botha at the Institute for Security studies (ISS) indicated that 87% of respondents gave religious conviction as the motivation why they joined Al Shabaab.

Andwhy do people who live a luxurious life in Europe and other parts of Western countries join terrorist organizations to battle in wars they most probably know little of? This is not an easy question to answer as there is no straightforward answer to it. Looking at the biographies of people who left Europe and North America to join extremist groups, we see that humanitarian considerations play a role. Here, pictures of human suffering in places like Syria have an effect but also the tendency to blame the west for not doing enough.

The second important point to think about is personal grievances. The majority young people that leave Europe to fight for extremist groups are angry, alienated and aggravated young men and women. They are ideologically dedicated to the cause and have embarked on a new life while totally putting behind their previous lives of comfort and luxury.

While there is a discussion on what constitutes terrorism and who a terrorist is, there is no doubt that children play a significant role and deliberate strategies have been formulated by terrorists to radicalize and recruit young people into committing violent acts.

In 1951, Eric Hoffer, a renowned author and lecturer, published a book, The True Believer, which was based upon his own observations of the rise of fascism, Nazism and communism as reactions to the Great Depression. He postulated that for the 'true believer' (someone committed to a cause that he or she is willing to thoughtlessly die for) it was the frustrations of life which led them to join a cause that gave meaning to their own existence. Justifiably, the more frustrated they felt, the more attracted and susceptible they were to extreme revolutionary solutions to their problems. This observation, made more than half a century ago, regrettably but accurately describes the dynamics and relations between youth and terrorism.

Owing to the expanding reach and propaganda of terrorist and violent extremist groups, child recruitment and exploitation is not limited to conflict area. More and more children are travelling from their countries of residence to areas controlled by terrorists and violent extremists group, in order to join them.

When recruiting children, terrorists and violent groups, as well as armed groups in general, benefit from notable economic advantage.

Whether they are used in support roles or combatants, children are usually paid less or nothing at all. Children are more easily intimidated and far easier to control, both physically and mentally, than adults. Children are more inclined to quickly show loyalty to authority figures and are especially susceptible to following beliefs and behaviors of those they love and respect an element that is especially relevant when families are involved in the recruitment process.

Estimates indicate that since, about 8,000 children have been forcibly recruited to and used for violent crimes by Boko Haram in Nigeria. According to a report by the United Nations Higher Commissioner for Human Rights, some boys have been forced to attack their own families to demonstrate loyalty to the terrorist group, while girls have been forced to marry, cook, and carry weapons. They are used as human shields in combat or as bomb detonators during suicide bombings. Boys are used to identify those who refused to join the group, as well as unmarried women and girls.

Refugee camps are breeding grounds for forcibly recruitment of young boys and girls into terrorism. An example of Kakuma Refugee Camp where boys and girls are not engaged in activities such as school going, terrorists groups lure such vulnerable children into joining terrorist groups with promises of financial support and travelling abroad for a better life. Refugee camps in Syria and Turkey are filled with young people separated from their parents. According to a new report by the British Think Tank Quilliam, these young refugees have become easy targets for recruitment by jihadist groups such as the "Islamic State" and are being sent to Europe. The UK-based think tank Quilliam foundation reported that the "Islamic State" or "IS" exploits the needs of children in refugee camps and their readiness to go to Europe and as such they recruit underage refugees boys and girls directly from the camps.

The recruitment of underage boys and girls is not just restricted to the camps but also to the areas that 'IS' controls. They have set up private schools to marshal and indoctrinate the children into joining them according to the European Center for Counterterrorism and Intelligence.

They use different methods to recruit minors and due to the children's difficult living conditions, they are easy targets for recruitment.

The 'Islamic State' lures the young refugees from their strongholds in Syria and Iraq where they exercise a type of influence over the children by giving them weapons and a good salary. In the camps, the Islamic State gives them money to go to Europe and plants extremist thoughts in their heads according to European Center for

Counterterrorism and Intelligence. They also pay smugglers a fee to transport the young refugees to Europe, which was referenced in the Quilliam report.

Prisons, also paradoxically, provide a contributory environment for terrorist recruitment. They are said to be the breeding grounds for radicalization and a places of vulnerability which due to the environment, produce identity seekers, protection seekers and rebels in huge numbers than in any other environment. The American criminologist, Harvey Kushner, argued that Western prisons were one of the main recruitment grounds for Al-Qaeda, while some have suggested that the relatively lax practices' in western prisons have been well exploited by Al-Qaeda. It is even worse when known terrorists are not separated from the juvenile population.

Violent armed groups such as the self-proclaimed Islamic State (ISIS), Boko Haram, and AlShabaab have increasingly targeted women and girls.

Regardless of the variations of the phenomenon, according to the international legal framework, the recruitment and exploitation of children by terrorists and violent groups are to be considered a serious form of violence against children.

The United Nations Office of Counter-Terrorism offers support of victims of terrorism. In its strategy it seeks to 'promote international solidarity in support of victims', stresses, 'the need to promote and protect the rights of victims of terrorism and their families and facilitate the normalization of their lives', and identifies the 'dehumanization of victims of terrorism' as one of the key issues that generates the conditions conducive to the spread of terrorism.

Despite the fact that Africa leads in forced recruitment of terrorists by terrorist groups, The African Union (AU) has remained on the sidelines. Only when Boko Haram became a trans-boundary threat, affecting neighbouring Chad and Cameroon, did the AU authorize a multinational force to deal with it.

The continental structure for counter-terrorism is mainly made up of the 1999 Organization of African Unity (OAU) Convention on the Prevention and Combating of Terrorism, supplemented in 2004 by a protocol, the AU Action Plan for the Prevention and Combating of Terrorism, and the mandate of the AU Special Representative for Counter-Terrorism Co-operation which was appointed in 2010.

Another barrier to action by the AU is the unconditional claims by member states regarding sovereignty and independence. This is even so in situations where these qualities of statehood are lacking. State measures remain the main instrument in the combating of terrorism and forced recruitment to terrorism.

The Story of Falma

14-year-old Falma told of how she escaped death by a whisker after she was sent on two separate suicide missions by two different sects of the lethal Boko Haram a deadly terrorist group in Nigeria; the largest country in Africa.

She narrated how she was first abducted by the insurgents at the age of 13 and managed to escape while she was on a suicide mission but ended up in the hands of yet another faction after which she was sent on a new suicide mission once again.

Following the abduction, the insurgents took her to a temporary make shift camp, where she also met other girls of her age or close to her age.

"The young girls were put in the tents. There were nine in mine and we had to sleep on big mats. At first I wanted to escape but there was no chance. We were so frightened that government soldiers would storm the camp at any time and kill all of us because they would think we were the fighters' wives,"

Falma said she was offered with two options: marry a fighter, or go on a mission but she had opted for the mission.

She narrated that during the stay in the makeshift camp of her first abductors, she was approached by armed men who gave her instructions to get ready for a very important mission.

"All that was running in my mind was, is it for marriage or what?' But you cannot question why? Instead other girls just comfort you to be patient."

Falma said she had a bomb tied around her waist area with strict instructions to go and kill non-believers.

"I was so frightened that I began to cry. I was told to be patient, and accept that this is what life is about".

Falma said she together with two other girls were strapped to explosives and were taken to the environs of a village. While armed with detonators, she and the other girls were ordered to walk towards the most populated areas for the assignment.

While on their way to her first suicide mission, she and the two other girls had decided against the attack and fled for safety. They then asked a stranger to help her take out the strap, and consequently ran away.

However she was not lucky. She ran out of luck as she was trying to flee the earlier suicide mission she met with two men, who belonged to a different faction of Boko Haram. She was consequently abducted again for the second time by the insurgents.

At the second camp, life was just the same with the previous one with the same practice, same beliefs and same destiny. After about a month, Falma was again offered with a choice – marriage to a fighter or suicide mission. Again, she settled for the suicide mission and shortly after they left her, Falma successfully escaped.

"I met some farmers and asked them to assist me take away the strap. I told them I was forced to carry out a suicide mission, but that I was not willing to do it".

They helped her get rid of the belt and she later joined a group of hunters who permitted her to move with them across the woods.

While trying to find her way back to the capital, and to her family, she and the group of hunters were ambushed by the insurgents. Fortunately, she managed to slip away into the forest.

"I didn't know the forest. Every little sound would scare me, but I kept moving. I'd sleep on trees at times. I think I spent a whole week with no food. I would drink stagnant water and also use this water to wash my hands and feet when praying. I would pray two or three times a day whenever I could find water. I was so scared, but God helped me and I reached a town."

A local family member later gave her protection for a few days to recuperate and gain her strength as they kept her hidden. Soon after, they helped her return back to her family.

The Story of Juma

Juma not his real name, 16 year old boy was walking on the streets of Nairobi in the sprawling slums of Kayole during the school holidays when he was abducted into a moving vehicle and blind folded to an unknown destination. While in the vehicle that is when he realized he was in the process of being recruited into a terrorist gang contrary to his thoughts that it would have been the usual abduction and ransom demands. Fearing for his life and the life of his family, Juma pretended to cooperate.

"As we continued driving through the streets, we passed through several police roadblocks oblivious to them of what was transpiring and who were the occupants in the vehicle. They were more interested on whether the vehicle was roadworthy and had all the required licenses to be on the road".

Juma was then frog matched into a giant mansion. It was his first time to be in such a house as he was used to his family one roomed iron sheet house he has grown to know as home. He does not remember the place. While there, he met other boys some as little as 12 years. Their parents were not aware of their whereabouts.

Two days later, he and the rest of the boys were bundled into a waiting car which had no registration number; they were driven for eight hours to an unknown town. He later realized that the place was Mombasa a coastal town in Kenya. From the accent of their language, he knew he was in Mombasa.

"On the red lights, I hoped that the police would stop and conduct a random check, but I was wrong".

While in Mombasa, Juma was promised 500 USD every month as monthly pay if he agreed to join the AlShaabab an extremist group predominant in the neighbouring country of Somalia that had its training camp in Somalia.

"The offer was too good but the thought of leaving my mother and brothers behind, not knowing

where I was as well as the thought of not going back to school was too much for me".

Juma cooperated with his kidnappers and acted as if he was in agreement with their arrangement. One day, before the departure date, the man manning the door fell asleep and that is when he and the other boys got the opportunity to escape.

"I ran as fast as I could, and luckily enough, I met two police officers who were on patrol. I explained everything that had happened, and how I got separated from my family. That is how my life was saved from being a terrorist, I am forever grateful".

*Fighting terrorism is a collective
responsibility.*

CHAPTER 9
LOST WITH NO TRACE

In international human rights law, a forced disappearance or enforced disappearance occurs when a person is secretly abducted or imprisoned by a state or political organization or by a third party with the authorization, support, or acquiesces of a state or political organization, followed by a refusal to acknowledge the person's fate and whereabouts, with the intent of placing the victim outside the protection of the law. A victim's lack of access to legal remedies puts them in a frightening and situation of complete defenselessness. Victims of enforced disappearance are also at heighted danger of other human rights violations, such as sexual violence or even murder.

Often than not, forced disappearance implies murder. The victim in such a case is abducted, detained illegally and sometimes subjected to torture during interrogation, and killed, with the body hidden never to be found. In some cases the victims live in constant fear of being killed. Characteristically, a murder will be mysterious, with the dead body disposed off to escape detection so that the person appears to have vanished. The party committing the murder has credible deniability, as nobody can provide evidence of the victim's death. Victims of enforced disappearance are individuals who have factually vanished from the society. They go missing when state officials (or someone acting with state consent) grabs them from the street or from their homes and then deny it, or refuse to disclose their whereabouts. Sometimes disappearances may be committed by armed non-state actors, like armed opposition groups and it is always a crime under international law.

Most often these people are never released and their fate remains mysterious. They know their families have no idea where they are and that there is little chance anyone is coming to help them. Even if they get lucky to escape death and are finally released, the physical and psychological scars stay with them.

Assessing the frequency of forced disappearance is difficult, but the practice seems to be becoming more widespread. Evidence from the Cingranelli and Richards Human Rights Database indicates the number of countries with 50 or more cases of forced disappearance almost doubled from 12 states in 2012 to 19 states in 2015 the most recent available comparable data.

As of September 2017, the United Nations Working Group on Enforced or Involuntary Disappearances which began collecting data in

1980 had a recording of 45,120 disappearance cases relating to 91 states.

It is unspeakable that state parties who are party to the International Convention and Political Rights, which guarantees people's rights to liberty and security and is monitored by the United Nations, are in fact more likely than not to commit conventional extrajudicial killings and forced disappearances.

Forced disappearances are well known instruments for human rights violators. The UN-sponsored truth commission for Guatemala estimated that up to 5,000 people disappeared during the country's civil war that lasted for 36 years; while in Argentina, campaigns to establish the fate of thousands of disappeared people continue to this day.

In Kenya, Haki Africa, a civil society organization accused the police of being behind extrajudicial killings and disappearances of people in the Coastal region in the past five years in the War on terrorism. While Kenya signed the International Convention for the Protection of All Persons from Enforced Disappearance (ICPPED), it has not ratified the Convention, and consequently the existing legal framework falls short of international human right standards, and is thus unable to comprehensively deal with the problem. It is estimated that in the last five years, over 110 persons have been forcefully disappeared. This number translates to 22 per year, which is almost two persons every month according to a 2018 report by Haki Africa. While a few of those disappeared at the Coast are linked to common crimes, including robbery with violence, the majority are suspected of terror-related crimes. The abductions are done in broad day light in public places as was the case of an 18-year-old

Juma Mbarak who was picked by unknown persons.

As he was being picked just in front of his father's garage, he managed to scream for help, which alerted his brother and co-workers. They rushed to the scene to find out what was happening, only to be repulsed by armed men who brandished their weapons and stated they were police officers doing their work. Juma was bundled into a waiting car, never to be seen again. Despite his father's and Haki Africa's relentless efforts to follow up with the authorities, there has been no trace of his whereabouts. The family is left destitute not knowing to weep or keep their hopes alive.

As a tool of terror, enforced disappearance is commonly applied as a strategy to instill fear within society. The feeling of insecurity and fear it generates is not restricted to the close relatives of the disappeared, but also affects communities and society at large.

A UN report notes Iraq has the largest number of disappearances, with more than 16,400 reported cases. Sri Lanka has more than 5,700 cases, Algeria more than 3,000 and El Salvador, Guatemala, and Peru each have more than 2,000 unresolved cases of enforced disappearances.

According to Amnesty International Report, Enforced disappearance is a global issue. Once mainly used by military dictatorships, disappearances now occur in almost every region in the world and in a wide range of contexts. They commonly occur in internal conflicts, mainly by governments trying to repress political opponents or by armed opposition groups.

Family and friends of people who have disappeared experience mental torture. The uncertainty of not knowing whether their son or daughter, mother or father is dead or alive is torturous. Not knowing where he or she is being held, or how they are being treated. Searching for the truth may put the whole family in great danger. Not knowing if their loved one will ever return often leaves their relatives living in limbo. According to research by Amnesty International and Human Rights Watch, the majority of victims of enforced disappearance are men yet it is women who most often lead the struggle to find out what happened in the minutes, days and years since the disappearance – putting themselves at risk of intimidation, persecution and violence.

To top it all off, the disappeared person is often the family's main breadwinner, the only one able to cultivate the crops or run the family business. This is then made worse by some national laws that don't let one draw a pension or receive other support without a death certificate.

The International Convention for the Protection
of All Persons from Enforced
Disappearance came into effect in 2010. It aims
to prevent enforced disappearances, uncover the
truth when they do happen and make sure
survivors and victims' families receive justice,
truth and reparation.

The Convention is one of strongest human rights
treaties ever adopted by the United Nations.
Unlike other crimes under international law,
such as torture, enforced disappearances were
not prohibited by a universal legally binding
instrument before the Convention came into force
in 2010.

The Convention provides a definition of the crime
of enforced disappearance and outlines necessary
state action in order to prevent both the
occurrence of the crime and to allow for the
investigation and prosecution of those who
perpetrate the act.

Implementation of the Convention is monitored by the Committee on Enforced Disappearances (CED). At the time of ratifying or acceding to the Convention, or even later, a state may declare that it recognizes the competence of CED to receive and consider communications from or on behalf of victims or other states parties. The CED also provides authoritative interpretations of the Convention.

The United Nations indicates that thousands of cases of enforced disappearances still remain unsolved. The U.N. Working Group on Enforced Disappearances says this atrocious practice continues unabated in every region of the world. The working group reported more than 43,000 cases from 88 countries still remain to be solved. While many of these cases are of recent period many date back decades.

While the world marks the annual international day in support of victims of enforced

162

disappearances, in many countries across the world, enforced disappearances are reported in various contexts but it's usually against a certain class of individuals. These could be from one religious group as is the case for Muslims in Myanmar, or ethnic minority as is the case for the Ormas in Ethiopia, or criminal suspects as is the case of drug addicts in Philippines and terror suspects in Kenya.

One common element of enforced disappearances is that it is persistent and one can draw a pattern over time considering the cases that are reported of the act in a given area. Enforced disappearance is in essence a violation of human dignity itself.

In Germany, a mass grave dating back from the Second World War and containing the bodies of at least 1,800 German men, women and children was unearthed by construction workers in northern Poland. The discovery was made in the town of Malbork, which was also known as Marienburg and was part of Germany during the Second World War, by the construction workers who were building a luxury hotel at the foot of the town's 13th-century fortress.

The bodies were assumed to be German civilians who disappeared after the Soviet army captured the town as it marched on Berlin in 1945. Many of the skulls were found with bullet holes in them, suggestive of executions that had taken place.

Polish and German experts concluded that they were the remains of German citizens still classified as missing persons. Many of the millions who disappeared in the pandemonium of wartime in Europe are still unaccounted for to date while the bodies were buried naked without any possessions.

Itai Dzamara

Itai Dzamara was one of the main outspoken critics of Robert Mugabe; former President of Zimbabwe, prior to his disappearance. Three years later, his loved ones are still waiting to resolve the mystery of his disappearance.

His wife and children have not seen him in more than three years since his disappearance. Their life has been hell on earth since the morning of 9 March 2015 when Mr. Dzamara was abducted.

Since then, they have lived a life in limbo full of anguish, uncertain whether he is still alive or is long dead and buried. Nonetheless, his wife has been strong for her ten-year-old son and five year old daughter.

"It's very hard for the children because they always ask about their father. You can really see that they miss him very much,"

In 2014, Mr. Dzamara began his one-man protest movement against the former president an

165

extremely dangerous path. During that time, Political dissenters often paid a heavy price including death. Challenging the President was unheard of.

But every single day, Mr. Dzamara went to sit in Africa Unity Square, a tree-filled park in the centre of Harare the capital city, holding his sign: "Failed Mugabe must step down."

Soon others began to join him.

His small acts of defiance came at a heavy price. In many occasions, Mr. Dzamara was beaten and severely injured by the police ending up in hospital recuperating from the wounds and the pain inflicted.

Taking his protest a notch higher, on 17 October 2014, Dzamara and two other protesters took their protest to the President's office to hand-deliver a petition to Mr. Mugabe asking him to step down.

They were detained, beaten and interrogated for eight hours. Less than six months afterward, Dzamara disappeared never to be found to date.

The events preceding his abduction are still very clear to the last person to see him who was his barber. That morning, he was working with another barber in their shop a short distance from Mr. Dzamara's house.

Mr. Dzamara was in the barber chair getting his beard trimmed when they noticed a white Nissan twin cab which seemed to be circling the block. Mr. Dzamara was positive he knew who the occupants were, noted one of the barber. *"Ndeye vakomana,"* he said - a Shona phrase meaning "it belongs to the boys".

"The boys" were Zimbabwe's secret police.

A few minutes later, two men clad in plain clothes walked in and asked to buy airtime for their mobile telephones.

When the barber said they did not sell airtime, the men later said they were in fact there for a cattle thief - Mr. Dzamara. He was handcuffed and bundled into the back of the car which sped off. He has not been seen since.

As to who abducted Mr. Dzamara and why is still a riddle. His brother believes "the ruling Zanu-PF and military intelligence" were behind it. The panic was that Mr. Dzamara would have been able to rally people into an uprising similar to the "Arab Spring".

The Zimbabwean government says it has no information about his abduction, detention or whereabouts.

The fall of Mr. Mugabe gave the family renewed hope in the search of Mr. Dzamara. A letter was sent to the administration of new President, Emmerson Mnanagwa, but as yet there has been no response. The Minister of Foreign Affairs, Sibusiso Moyo, talked to BBC and said that the days of abductions were long over and the new government respects the lives of every Zimbabwean.

*"It pains me. When I see his picture, I start crying, "*Mr. Dzamara's friend says, his voice breaking.*"They should just give him a decent burial. If they have killed him they must just give us back his remains."*

Enforced Disappearances in Mexico

Mexico City security forces have participated in widespread enforced disappearances according to a report by Human Rights report released in 2013. Virtually none of the victims have been found or those responsible brought to justice, exacerbating the suffering of families of the disappeared.

A 176-page report, "Mexico's Disappeared: *The Enduring Cost of a Crisis Ignored"* documents almost 250 "disappearances" during the administration of former President Felipe Calderón, from December 2006 to December 2012. In 149 of those cases, Human Rights Watch found compelling evidence of enforced disappearances, involving the participation of state agents.

Human Rights Watch (a non-profit, non-governmental human rights organization) found evidence that members of all branches of the security forces carried out enforced disappearances: the Army, the Navy, and the federal and local police. In some cases, such as a series of more than 20 enforced disappearances by Navy personnel in June and July 2011 in Nuevo León and Tamaulipas, the common *modus operandi* of the crimes, the scale of the operations, and the inconsistent accounts by the Navy suggest the crimes may have been planned and coordinated.

In over 60 cases, Human Rights Watch found evidence that state agents collaborated directly with organized crime groups to "disappear" people and extort payments from their families. For example, evidence indicates that local police in Pesquería, Nuevo León arbitrarily detained 19 construction workers in May 2011 and handed them over to an organized crime group. The men have not been seen since.

The nearly 250 disappearances documented in the report do not represent all of the cases in Mexico since 2007. On the contrary, official statistics leave little doubt that there are thousands more. A provisional list compiled by the Federal Prosecutor's Office and the Interior Ministry of more than 25,000 people who were "disappeared" or reported missing since 2006 was leaked to the media in November 2012. Prosecutors and law enforcement officials consistently fail to search thoroughly and promptly for people reported missing or to investigate those responsible for the disappearances. All too often, these officials blame the victims and tell families it is their responsibility to investigate, Human Rights Watch found. What limited steps prosecutors take are undermined by recurring delays, errors, and omissions.

In none of the 249 cases documented by Human Rights Watch have the people responsible been convicted for carrying out disappearances.

The incompetent or altogether absent investigations worsen the suffering of the families, for whom not knowing what happened to their loved ones is a source of continuous torment. Making matters worse, families of the disappeared may lose access to basic social services that are tied to the victim's employment, forcing them to fight slow, costly, and emotionally draining battles to restore essential benefits such as child care.

Luz María Durán Mota whose 17-year-old son, Israel Arenas Durán, was disappeared together with three coworkers in Monterrey, Nuevo León after being detained by local police in June 2011 – told Human Rights Watch, "It is a daily torture, not knowing where he is. If they are torturing him or if he's had anything to eat."

Efforts by the Calderón administration to address this problem were belated and grossly inadequate. For most of his presidency, Calderón denied that security forces had committed human rights violations. In his last year, he acknowledged that abuses had occurred and pledged to take steps to address them. But he did not fulfill most of his commitments, such as completing a national registry of the disappeared, or submitting a new legislative proposal to Congress to reform the Code of

Military Justice that complied with four rulings on the issue by the Inter-American Court of Human Rights.

The report also documents examples of positive steps at the state level to address disappearances. In Nuevo León, government officials and prosecutors, responding to pressure from victims' families and human rights defenders, have begun to investigate seriously a select group of approximately 50 disappearance cases. While progress so far has been limited, and only a few disappeared people have been found, the collaborative effort shows how winning back the trust of victims' families and empowering them to hold prosecutors accountable can help overcome some of the greatest obstacles to investigations.

Ultimately, the success of state-level efforts will depend largely on whether the federal government takes steps to address the problem.

More examples of disappearances featured in the report in which evidence strongly suggests the involvement of security forces includes ten men from Guanajuato were illegally detained in December 2011 by local police in the municipality of Joaquín Amaro, Zacatecas as they returned from a hunting trip. According to two members of the group who escaped, police officers blindfolded, beat, and interrogated the men about whether they had ties to organized crime. Security camera footage shows local police later handed eight of the detainees to armed men at a gas station in Fresnillo, Zacatecas. The eight men were never seen again.

José Fortino Martínez Martínez was arbitrarily detained at his home in Nuevo Laredo, Tamaulipas in June 2011 by men wearing Navy uniforms, as members of his family looked on. Relatives of Martínez and other men abducted that night took photographs and video footage of the vehicles that participated in the detentions, which bear Navy insignia. In July, Martínez' wife met with federal prosecutors and representatives of the Ministry of the Interior to request investigations into her husband's disappearance. Three days later, her home was sprayed with bullets.

Roberto Iván Hernández García and Yudith Yesenia Rueda García, both age 17, were abducted from the home of Rueda's grandmother in Monterrey, Nuevo León, on March 11, 2011, by men wearing federal police uniforms. Several family members witnessed their illegal detention. Approximately a week later, a man came to Hernández's home and warned a relative that if the family wanted to avoid more children being taken, they should not report the case to authorities. Hernández and Rueda have not been seen since.

Oscar Germán Herrera Rocha, Ezequiel Castro Torrecillas, Sergio Arredondo Sicairos, and Octavio del Billar Piña all called their spouses separately to tell them they had been stopped by local police at a gas station in Francisco I. Madero, Coahuila in May 2009. They were never seen again. Three people disappeared in identical circumstances in the same location the previous month.

Governments have a legal and moral

obligation to curb enforced

disappearances

CHAPTER 10
PAINS FROM HOME

When pain and suffering happens in a familiar territory you have known as home for many years and is perpetrated by those that should be protecting you, considering you as unwanted and must be "finished", then you wonder where humanity is! Has it been thrown to the dogs? The United Nations described the mass exodus of Rohingya Muslims from Mynamar as "the world's fastest growing refugee crisis and a textbook example of ethnic cleansing.

Ethnic cleansing has been defined by a United Nations Commission of Experts mandates to look into violations of international humanitarian law committed in the territory of the former Yugoslavia as the attempt to get rid of through deportation, displacement or even mass killing members of an unwanted ethnic group in order to establish an ethnically homogenous geographic area. Though cleansing campaigns for ethnic or religious reasons have existed throughout history, the rise of extreme national movements during the 20th century led to an unprecedented level of ethnically motivated brutality, including the recent Rohingya massacre in Mynamar, Turkish massacre of Armenians during World War 1, the Nazis' annihilation of some 6 million European Jews in the Holocaust and the forced displacement and mass killings carried out in the former Yugoslavia and African country of Rwanda during the 1990's.

While the Rohingya have been persecuted by the Myanmar for decades, the situation has greatly escalated in the past five years. In 2012 revenge attacks against Muslims in the region intensified after the rape and murder of a Buddhist woman by Rohingyas. The following year, Buddhists men coordinated attacks on Muslim villages in Rakhine state, which is the home of most of the Rohingya. The Human Rights Watch noted that the brutality was a synchronized drive to forcibly relocate or remove the state's Muslims.

The International Criminal Court (ICC) has linked ethnic cleansing more specifically to genocide, crimes against humanity and war crimes as ethnic cleansing has not been recognized as an independent crime under international law. The coercive practices used to remove the civilian population may include murder, torture, arbitrary arrest and detention, extrajudicial executions, rape and sexual assaults, severe physical injury to civilians, confinement of civilian population in ghetto areas, forcible removal, displacement and deportation of civilian population, deliberate military attacks on civilians and civilian areas, use of civilian as human shields, destruction of property, robbery of personal property, attacks on hospitals, medical personnel, and locations with the Red Cross/Rd Crescent emblem, among others.

Ethnic cleansing as a notion has generated considerable argument. Critics see little difference between it and genocide. Defenders, however, argue that ethnic cleansing and genocide can be distinguished by the intent of the perpetrator; whereas the primary goal of genocide is the purging of an ethnic, racial, or religious group, the main purpose of ethnic cleansing is the establishment of ethnically homogeneous lands, which may be achieved by any of a number of methods including genocide.

During the Rwandan genocide of 1994, members of the Hutu ethnic majority in the east-central African nation of Rwanda murdered as many as 800,000 people, mostly Tutsi minority. Started by

Hutu nationalists in the capital of Kigali, the genocide spread throughout the country with shocking speed and brutality, as ordinary citizens were incited by local officials and the Hutu Power government to take up arms against their neighbours. By the time the Tutsi-led Rwandese Patriotic Front gained control of the country through a military offensive in early July, hundreds of thousands of Rwandans were dead and 2 million refugees mainly Hutus fled Rwanda, exacerbating what had already become a full blown humanitarian crisis.

The Rwanda genocide has been compared to the Nazi Holocausts in its bizarre cruelty. But there is a fundamental difference between these two atrocities; no Jewish army posed a threat to Germany. Hitler targeted the Jews and other weak groups solely because of his own demented beliefs and the prevailing prejudices of the time. The Rwandan Hutu *genocidaires*, as the people who killed during the genocide were known, were also motivated by absurd beliefs and prejudices.

Three and a half years before the genocide, a rebel army mainly Rwandan Tutsi exiles known as the Rwandan Patriotic Front or RPF, had invaded Rwanda and set up camps in the northern mountains. They had been armed and trained be neighbouring Uganda, which continued to supply them throughout the ensuing civil war, in violation of the UN carter, Organization of African Unity rules, various Rwandan ceasefire and peace agreements, and the repeated promises of the Ugandan president, Yoweri Museveni.

Despite all the persecutions happening globally, the ICC's hands are tied and hence perpetrators go scot free as not every country is a signatory to the ICC, and you need to be a signatory in order for the court to have jurisdiction. Myanmar is not a signatory.

Violence against women, particularly rape, has added its own brand of indignity to recent wars. From conflicts in Bosnia and Herzegovina to Peru to Rwanda, girls and women have been singled out for defilement, rape, incarceration, torture and execution. Rape, defined by psychologists as the most intrusive of traumatic events, has been documented in many armed conflicts and wars both intra and inter conflicts including those in Bangladesh, Cambodia, Cyprus, Haiti, Liberia, Somalia and Uganda. Organized rape is often used as a weapon of war in 'ethnic cleansing'. More than 20,000 Muslim girls and women have been raped in Bosnia since fighting began in April 1992, according to a European Community fact-finding team. Teenage girls have been a particular target in Bosnia and Herzegovina and Croatia, according to The State of the World's Children 1996 report. The report also says that impregnated girls have been forced to put up with 'the enemy's' child.

In some attacks in Rwanda, almost every adolescent girl who survived an attack by the militia was subsequently raped. Many of those who became pregnant were not accepted by their families and communities. Some abandoned their babies; while others committed suicide to run away from the disgrace and embarrassment.

Sexual violation of women erodes the fabric of a community in a way that few weapons can. Rape's damage can be devastating due to the strong communal reaction to the violation and anguish stamped on families of the victims. The harm inflicted in such cases on a woman by a rapist is an attack on her family and culture, as in many societies women are viewed as repositories of the society's cultural and religious values.

In addition to rape, girls and women are also subject to forced prostitution and trafficking during times of war, sometimes with the complicity of governments and military authorities. During World War II, women were abducted, imprisoned and forced to satisfy the sexual needs of occupying forces, and many Asian women were also involved in prostitution during the Viet Nam war. The tendency continues in today's conflicts.

The State of the World's Children 1996 report notes that the disintegration of families in times of war leaves women and girls especially vulnerable to violence. Nearly 80 per cent of the 53 million people uprooted by wars today are women and children. When fathers, husbands, brothers and sons are drawn away to fight, they leave women, the very young and the elderly to fend for themselves. In Bosnia and Herzegovina, Myanmar and Somalia, refugee families frequently cite rape or the fear of rape as a key factor in their decisions to seek refuge.

During the Mozambique's war, young boys, who themselves had been traumatized by violence, were reported to threaten to kill or starve girls if they resisted the boys' sexual advances. Sexual assault presents a major problem in camps for refugees and the displaced, according to the report. The incidence of rape was reported to be alarmingly high at camps for Somali refugees in Kenya in 1993. The camps were located in isolated areas, and hundreds of women were raped in night raids or while foraging for firewood.

UNHCR (the Office of the UN High Commissioner for Refugees) has had to organize security patrols, fence camps with thorn bushes and relocate the most vulnerable women to safer areas. Some rape victims who were detested were moved to other camps or given priority for resettlement abroad. UNHCR has formal guidelines for preventing and responding to sexual violence in the camps, and it trains field workers to be more sensitive to victims' needs. Refugee women are encouraged to form community groups and become involved in camp administration to make them less vulnerable to men who would steal their supplies or force them to provide sex in return for provisions.

The high risk of infection with sexually transmitted diseases (STDs), including HIV/AIDS, accompanies all sexual violence against women and girls. The movement of refugees and prowling military units and the breakdown of health services and public education worsens the impact of diseases and likelihood for treatment. For example, one study has suggested that the exchange of sex for protection during the civil war in Uganda in the

1980s was a causative factor to the country's high rate of AIDS.

War and civil unrest also contribute to violence in the home, according to recent studies. Death, turmoil and poverty increase tensions within the family and the likelihood of violence against girls and women. Men who feel that they have lost the ability to protect their women may compensate by exercising violent control over them at home.

UNHCR, the United Nations Population Fund (UNFPA) and UNICEF are promoting reproductive health services for refugees to counter high birth rates, maternal mortality, STDs and HIV/AIDS. UNICEF provides support for women affected by armed conflict in countries such as Bosnia and Herzegovina, Burundi, Croatia, Georgia, Liberia, Rwanda, Somalia and the Sudan.

The post-World War II Nuremberg trials condemned rape as a crime against humanity.

Governments must show commitment and be willing to enforce international law and codes of conduct, while also supporting counseling and other services for victims.

The Rohingya

Stories of rape, murder and scorched earth is a daily thing for the Rohingya in Myanmar.

***"They grabbed my baby out of my arms and threw her into a fire, and she burned to death".*-Rajuma**

Rajuma was 20 years old when she fled from the northern Rakhine state in Myanmar to Bangladesh after her village of Tula Toli was destroyed and liquidated by Burmese forces.

She narrated how on August 30th, soldiers stormed into Tula Toli, set homes on fire, and led villagers down to river where they separated women from the men. The men cried out to the soldiers begging for their lives to be spared but to no sympathy. They were all executed. It was that the soldiers turned their attention to Rajuma, who had brought her infant girl with her.

"They grabbed my baby out of my arms and threw her into a fire, and she burned to death".

Rajuma was then hit in the face with a club, and the soldiers gang-raped her in her home along with her two sisters. All her relatives were murdered. She then fled her village naked and her body covered with blood in order to join other Rohingya who were making their way to safety in the neighbouring Bangladesh.

Ayesha was also raped by 12 soldiers in September on 2017.

"I don't remember how many of them raped me, but at one point, I had lost consciousness from my fading screams".

The Story of Marjorie

Marjorie is a survivor of the Rwandan genocide. She was the ninth of ten children in her family.

"The massacre began on the 11th April 1994 in our home area. There was so much noise and shouting so we decided to leave the house, but we were ordered to go to the area district office. I later learnt that our house was torched down"

At the District office, they spent the next three days without food or water. The Interahamwe militia was in control and closed the all water points so that they could die for lack of water. The Interahamwe was a Hutu paramilitary organization originally the youth wing of ruling party of Rwanda, the MRND, during the Rwandan Genocide the phrase "Interahamwe" widened to mean any civilian bands killing Tutsi. The militia enjoyed the backing of the Hutu-led government leading up to and during the genocide. Since the genocide, they have been driven out of Rwanda, mainly to Zaire (present day Democratic Republic of the Congo). They are considered a terrorist organization by most Western governments, as well as several countries in Africa (including Rwanda, the Democratic Republic of the Congo, and several others).

"If someone tried to leave to go look for food, they were shot dead"

On the third day, two trucks full of the Interahamwe militia and soldiers arrived carrying grenades and guns. That is when the massacre began. Some of the men tried to defend themselves using stones, but because they were fighting against guns and grenades, it was obvious that there was no way they could win. Many of them were killed. Marjorie lost her father, her three brothers, two cousins and an uncle in the massacre. Those that survived the grenades explosions were killed using machetes.

"There were so many of us, that they did not have enough bullets to kill all of us and so they left warning us not to leave as they will be coming back to finish the job. We then decided to flee to another place for safety. We needed to cross a lake to get there but my father's boat, which we intended to use, had been destroyed. We sat down because we could not do anything. We were helpless, as death was everywhere. Some of us managed to swim across others opted to commit suicide".

They finally arrived at a house where they sought refuge. The woman there was frightened since her house was also a target for attack and so they could not stay there. They went to the bush where they spent three days without food or water.

"The woman would come to see us, and finally took us to her neighbour who was willing to continue hiding us. While there, I learnt from the lady that my mother had been killed. My young sister was with her but was lucky to escape with an injury"

Her mother was buried in a shallow grave and her sister was left beside the grave for three days to die a slow death. She was four years old at the time. When she regained consciousness, she went to ask for shelter from the neighbours but they refused. She then went to the house whose owners were related to the people who were hiding her and who had also sent a message that she should go pick her sister from their house.

"I was so much pained seeing my sister in that condition. She was coughing and spitting out blood. She couldn't eat, or speak but she recognized me.

The militia would check from house to house looking for people to kill. We had to hide in the bush near the house from 5am to 8pm. During the night we went back to the house. We lived in these conditions until the month of June".

As the war advanced, the killers discovered their hiding place. They were all taken to a certain house where the girls were raped everyday by the militia.

Marjorie tested positive to HIV as a result of the rapes she endured during the genocide. She discontinued school as she was not financially able to pay for her own school fees. Her parents perished in the genocide. She is now a survivor though battling the disease with very little resources. She lives with her brother who supports her for all her needs.

The Story of Monica

Monica is a Hutu woman who was married to a Tutsi man. During the genocide her family was attacked by her own brothers and father.

"I was forced to witness the slaughtering of my six children and husband with a blunt machete to ensure that they experienced maximum pain".

She could hear their screams of pain and terror. Her father was screaming at her that it was her fault that the family was murdered as she was married to a 'snake', the local phrase describing a Tutsi.

"I ran away to the neighbouring country of Tanzania where I lived in a refugee camp. My father was also there but we never spoke".

All her brothers were sent to jail for the atrocious crimes they committed during the genocide.

"The cause of the genocide was mere ungrounded hatred, how else could you explain families

murder their own family members? I still do not understand the hatred to date".

Monica put everything that happened behind her. She forgave those who killed her family, friends and neighbours. She remarried and now has two beautiful children.

*Perpetrators of crimes against
humanity should be punished.*

Key References

- The U.S. State Department's annual report of Human Rights Practices.
- The United Nations' annual background note on Gender Equality, Nationality Laws and Statelessness.
- References to official country-specific government websites.
- Female Genital Mutilation/Cutting: A Global Concern (UNICEF) 2016
- World Health Organization, Female Genital Mutilation published 31/01/208
- Working towards Zero tolerance for female genital mutilation in Sudan.
- End FGM European Network 26/08/2016
- International Day of Zero Tolerance for Female Genital Mutilation-African Union
- How my mother circumcised me then married me off to a 60 year old; Nairobi wire, Thursday, 14 Nov 2013.
- CNN.com (2009) Lawyer fights widow sex tradition in Malawi
- Allafrica.com (2007). Kenya. Bizarre widow cleansing ritual.

- Paul Frimpong-Electoral Violence in Africa, Causes; Implications and Solutions Dec 1,2012
- UNODC Handbook on children recruited and exploited by terrorist and violent groups.
- The Lure of Youth into Terrorism by Thoma Koruth Samuel.
- Rodwan Abouharb Forced disappearances are on the rise as human rights violators cover their tracks.
- United Nation-Genocide Prevention and the Responsibility to Protect.
- Syracuse Journal of International Law and Commerce; The Rohingya and International Laws of Ethnic Cleansing.
- Amnesty International www.amnestyinternational.org
- BBC; Itai Dzamara: The man who stood up to Zimbabwe's Robert Mugabe and vanished 24/05/2018
- Human Rights Watch Mexico: Crisis of Enforced Disappearances 2013
- 14-yr-old girl escapes suicide mission twice after abduction. Published: 10.02.2018 Gbenga Bada

- The State of the World's Children 1996
  UNICEF.

ABOUT THE AUTHOR

Benedetta Wasonga, born in Hola, a small village in the Coast province is a communications, human rights and gender specialist. She received her Masters degree (MA) in human rights, Bachelor of Arts Degree in Armed Conflict and Peace Studies, Communication and Psychology from the University of Nairobi and a Diploma in Law. She has trained in Business Management at the Kenya Institute of Management**(KIM)** Nairobi, Leadership Development Programme for Enhanced Public Service Delivery at the Administrative Staff College of India **(ASCI)** in Hyderabad Indiaand Corporate Social Responsibility and Accountability Programme at the Eastern and Southern African Management Institute **(ESAMI)** in Arusha Tanzania.

She has experience working with refugees at Kakuma Refugee Camp with the Ministry of Interior and Coordination of National Government; Directorate of Immigration and Registration of persons and as a legal researcher in various law firms and a vast experience in policy drafting and implementation such as Workplace HIV Policy, The KFS Corporate Social Responsibility and Accountability Policy 2016, Gender Equality Policy.

She has written various research work on promotion and protection of children's rights to education and articles such the Curse of Corruption, Environmental Human Rights; A Claim Right for All, African Union, Hope for the African People, Population Growth; a Human Rights Concern among others. She is currently working on her next book *"The Killer Candy"* which talks about the devastation drug abuse has caused on various aspects of social and economic development and the role of governments and societies in supporting victims and their families instead of victimization and discrimination.

She is member of African Women's Development
and Communications Network (FEMNET).

wbenedetta@gmail.com